OLD TOWN
Pages 8–17

NEW TOWN
Pages 60–69

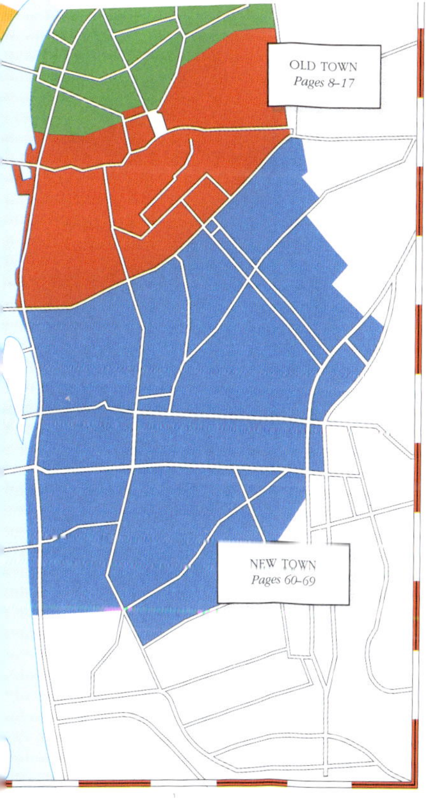

EYEWITNESS TRAVEL
PRAGUE
POCKET GUIDE

LONDON, NEW YORK,
MELBOURNE, MUNICH AND DELHI
www.dk.com

PROJECT DIRECTORS Nicholas Bevan, Derek Hall

EDITORS Derek Hall, Marion Dent, Alexander Stillwell

DESIGNER Tony Truscott

INDEXER Michael Dent

PICTURE RESEARCHER Mirco De Cet

CARTOGRAPHY John Plumer, Dave Brooker, Paul Hopgood

Conceived and produced by Redback Publishing, 25 Longhope Drive, Farnham, Surrey, GU10 4SN
Reproduced by Colourscan (Singapore)
Printed and bound by Leo Paper Products Ltd. in China
First published in Great Britain in 2006
by Dorling Kindersley Limited
80 Strand, London WC2R 0RL

Reprinted with revisions 2008, 2010

Copyright 2006, 2010 © Dorling Kindersley Limited, London
A Penguin Company

ALL RIGHTS RESERVED. NO PART OF THIS PUBLICATION MAY BE REPRODUCED, STORED IN A RETRIEVAL SYSTEM, OR TRANSMITTED IN ANY FORM OR BY ANY MEANS, ELECTRONIC, MECHANICAL, PHOTOCOPYING, RECORDING OR OTHERWISE, WITHOUT THE PRIOR WRITTEN PERMISSION OF THE COPYRIGHT OWNER.

A CIP CATALOGUE RECORD IS AVAILABLE FROM THE BRITISH LIBRARY.

ISBN: 978-1-40535-401-1

MIX
Paper from
responsible sources
FSC™ C018179

The information in this
DK Eyewitness Travel Guide is checked regularly.

Every effort has been made to ensure that this book is as up-to-date as possible at the time of going to press. Some details, however, such as telephone numbers, opening hours, prices, gallery hanging arrangements and travel information, are liable to change. The publishers cannot accept responsibility for any consequences arising from the use of this book, nor for any material on third-party websites, and cannot guarantee that any website address in this book will be a suitable source of travel information. We value the views and suggestions of our readers highly. Please write to:
Publisher, DK Eyewitness Travel Guides,
Dorling Kindersley, 80 Strand, London WC2R 0RL.

View over the rooftops to Prague Castle, dominating the city of Prague

CONTENTS

INTRODUCING PRAGUE

Central Prague **4**

Prague Highlights **6**

Town Hall Clock, Old Town

PRAGUE AREA BY AREA

Old Town **8**

Jewish Quarter **18**

Prague castle and Hradčany **28**

Little Quarter **44**

New Town **60**

Farther Afield **70**

PRACTICAL INFORMATION

Getting Around **74**

Survival Guide **76**

Index **78**

Acknowledgments **80**

Baroque lion (1730) with winged cherub, outside the Royal Garden

Central Prague

The River Vltava bisects this glorious city, with the wonders of Prague Castle and the Little Quarter on one side, and the Old and New Towns and the Jewish Quarter on the other. These fascinating areas are connected by the magnificent Charles Bridge with its superb sculpted statues of saints.

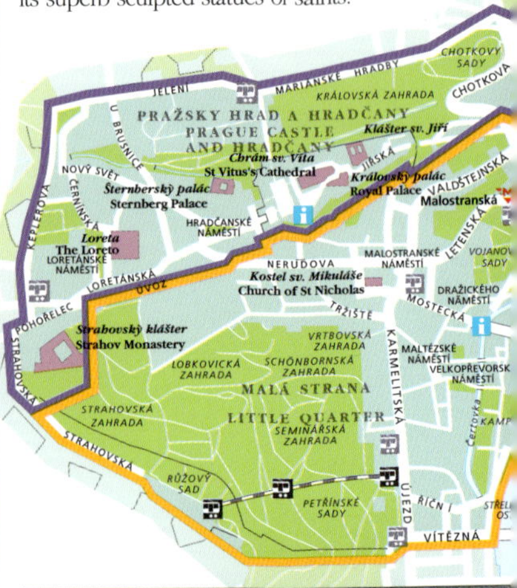

KEY

Metro station	
Coach station	
Tram stop	
Funicular railway	
River boat boarding point	
Tourist information	

View of Prague Castle and St Vitus's Cathedral

From the glorious edifice of Prague Castle, St Vitus's Cathedral dominates this panoramic view (see p30).

0 metres 250
0 yards 250

CENTRAL PRAGUE

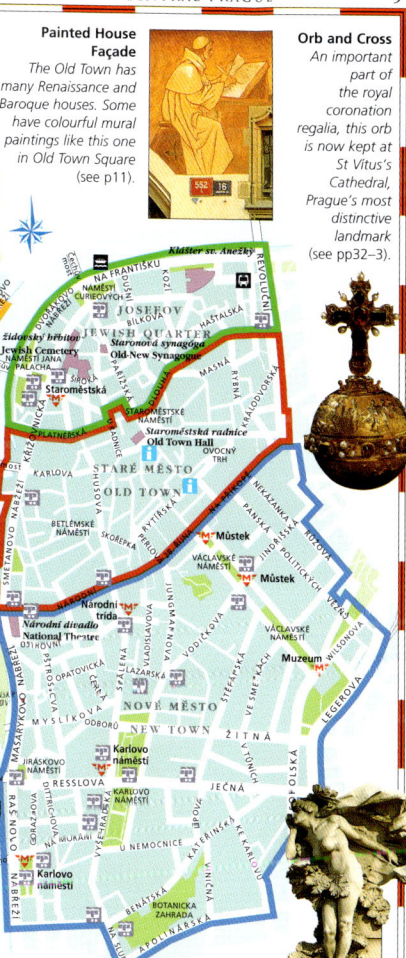

Painted House Façade
The Old Town has many Renaissance and Baroque houses. Some have colourful mural paintings like this one in Old Town Square (see p11).

Orb and Cross
An important part of the royal coronation regalia, this orb is now kept at St Vitus's Cathedral, Prague's most distinctive landmark (see pp32–3).

Art Nouveau Statue
The New Town has many examples of Art Nouveau architecture (see p61).

Prague's Highlights

Prague's beautiful cityscape has been carved by emperors, artists and religious communities. Enjoy its Gothic castle and cathedral, medieval Jewish Cemetery and the opulent New Town. Here is a time-saving guide to the best Prague has to offer.

Whale skeleton, National Museum

Museums and Galleries

National Gallery
Extensive art collection in several locations: Kinský Palace: prints and drawings (see p11); St Agnes Convent: medieval (see p27); St George's Convent: Baroque (see p31); Sternberg Palace: Old Masters (see p38); and Veletržní Palace: modern.

Picture Gallery of Prague Castle
Fine collection of paintings and sculptures from the 16th–18th century (see p30).

National Museum
Devoted mainly to natural history, minerals and archaeology (see pp62–3).

Jewish Museum
Perhaps the world's largest collection of Judaic art can be seen in six of the Jewish Quarter's synagogues: Old-New (see pp24–5), Pinkas, Klausen, Maisel, High (see p21) and Spanish (see p26).

Smetana Museum
Remembering the famous Czech composer's life and work by the River Vltava (see p17).

Churches and Synagogues

St Vitus's Cathedral
The jewel of this glorious Gothic cathedral, towering high above Prague Castle, is the magnificent Chapel of St Wenceslas (see p32).

Old-New Synagogue
Prague's Orthodox Jewish community still holds services in Europe's oldest synagogue, which dates from 1270 (see pp24–5).

The Loreto
The treasury of one of Prague's finest Baroque buildings contains fabulous liturgical items (see p36).

Strahov Monastery
A working monastery from 1140, it houses the nation's oldest books (see pp40–41).

Church of St Nicholas
This High Baroque masterpiece is magnificently decorated with statues, frescoes and paintings (see pp48–9).

Dome of Church of St Nicholas, Prague's finest High Baroque sight

PRAGUE'S HIGHLIGHTS

Art Nouveau

Zbraslav Monastery
Marvellous Art Nouveau pieces proliferate in the sculpture gardens (see p73).

Hotel Europa
This splendid hotel's highly decorated façade with gilded nymphs and the superb interior of panelling and mirrors are just some of its many Art Nouveau features (see p62).

The Hotel Europa has a wealth of fine Art Nouveau details inside and out

Municipal House
The interior of Prague's star Art Nouveau attraction is superbly decorated with works by leading early 20th-century Czech artists, including the renowned Alfons Mucha (see p10).

Museum of Decorative Arts
Five centuries of arts and crafts are on show, with impressive collections of glass, furniture and graphic art, including many fine Art Nouveau gems (see p20).

Mucha Museum
One of the most successful exponents of the Art Nouveau movement, artist and national hero Alfons Mucha is justly renowned for his celebrated posters, also jewellery, furniture, stained glass and even postage stamps (see p63).

Palaces and Gardens

Royal Palace and Garden
Dating from 1135, this intriguing building has three architectural layers, Romanesque, Gothic and Renaissance. Two Baroque lions guard the garden's entrance (see p30 and p35).

Belvedere
Formerly called the Royal Summer Palace, this fine Italian Renaissance building sports a "Singing Fountain" in the front (see p35).

South Gardens
Several small gardens link up to occupy the narrow band of land below Prague Castle overlooking the Little Quarter (see p34).

Petřín Park
Escape the city crowds and enjoy the magnificent panoramas of Prague from the 300-m (1,000-ft) slopes of Petřín hill (see p58).

Wallenstein Palace and Garden
This vast Baroque edifice was intended to outshine Prague Castle. Its stunning main hall is two storeys high, while the gardens have a fountain and rows of bronze statues (see p46).

Wallenstein Garden's statues are copies of 17th-century bronzes

OLD TOWN
STARÉ MĚSTO

The heart of the city is the Old Town. Architecturally, it embraces every epoch from Romanesque onwards. The Town Hall, Clam-Gallas Palace and Municipal House reflect the area's importance, while its cafés, clubs and restaurants keep the district buzzing.

SIGHTS AT A GLANCE

Churches
Church of St James ❸
Church of Our Lady before Týn ❼
Church of St Nicholas ❾
Church of St Gall ⓬
Church of St Martin in the Wall ⓭
Church of St Giles ⓯

Museums and Galleries
Náprstek Museum ⓮
Smetana Museum ㉑

Historic Streets and Squares
Old Town Square ❻
Mariánské Square ⓱
Charles Street ⓲
Knights of the Cross Square ㉒

Historic Monuments and Buildings
Powder Gate ❶
Municipal House ❷

Carolinum ❺
Old Town Hall pp14–15 ❿
House at the Two Golden Bears ⓫
Clementinum ⓴

Theatres
Estates Theatre ❹

Palaces
Kinský Palace ❽
Clam-Gallas Palace ⓰
Palace of the Lords of Kunštát ⓳

SEE ALSO

• *Street Life p17*

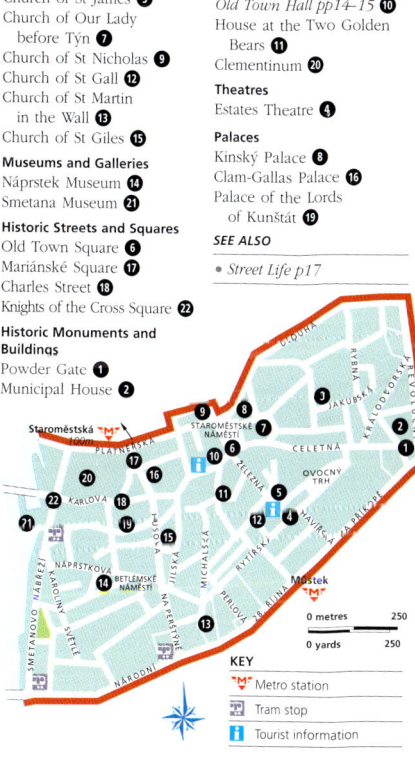

KEY
Ⓜ Metro station
🚋 Tram stop
ⓘ Tourist information

◀ *Mucha's allegory of Vigilance in the Municipal House*

The Powder Gate viewed from outside the Old Town

Powder Gate ❶
PRAŠNÁ BRÁNA

Map 3H. Náměstí Republiky. Open daily Apr–Oct. Adm charge.

The monumental entrance to the Old Town was built in the Gothic style by Matěj Rejsek in 1475. Used to store gunpowder in the 1600s (hence its name), its rich sculptural decoration was badly damaged by Prussian forces in 1757. The Neo-Gothic façade seen today dates from 1876.

Municipal House ❷
OBECNÍ DŮM

Map 3H. Náměstí Republiky 5. Open daily. Adm charge.

The most striking feature of Prague's star Art Nouveau sight is Karel Špillar's huge semi-circular mosaic above the main entrance, entitled *Homage to Prague*. The interior is decorated with works by leading Czech artists, including Alfons Mucha. Also inside, topped by an impressive glass dome, is Smetana Hall, Prague's principal concert venue. It was from Municipal House that Czechoslovakia was declared an independent state in 1918.

Church of St James ❸
KOSTEL SV. JAKUBA

Map 3G. Malá Štupartská. Open in the season, Mon–Sat. Free.

This attractive church was restored to new Baroque glory after a fire in 1689. Typical of its grandeur is a 16th-century wooden Pietà and a magnificent organ built in 1702. Over 20 side altars are decorated with works by renowned Czech artists. Of macabre note is the 400-year-old mummified arm of a thief above the entrance.

Baroque organ loft in the Church of St James

Estates Theatre ❹
STAVOVSKÉ DIVADLO

Map 4G. Ovocný trh 1. Foyer open daily.

One of the finest examples of Neo-Classical elegance in Prague, the theatre is a mecca for Mozart fans. In 1787, *Don Giovanni* had its debut here, with Mozart at the piano conducting the orchestra.

OLD TOWN

Statue of the Madonna on the Church of Our Lady before Týn

Carolinum 5
KAROLINUM

Map 4G. Ovocný trh 3. Open for special exhibitions only.

At the core of the university, founded in 1348, is the Carolinum. The chapel, arcade and walls survive, together with a magnificently carved oriel window, but the courtyard was reconstructed in 1945.

Old Town Square 6
STAROMĚSTSKÉ NÁMĚSTÍ

Map 3F.

This square is the very heart and soul of Prague. The east side boasts the Church of Our Lady before Týn and the stunning Rococo Kinský Palace, while the north side is dominated by the Baroque Church of St Nicholas. Colourful Romanesque and Gothic houses grace the south side.

Church of Our Lady before Týn 7
KOSTEL MATKY BOŽÍ PŘED TÝNEM

Map 3G. Týnská, Štupartská. Open Mon–Fri. Free.

This magnificent church looms over the Old Town Square's dainty houses. A gold statue of the Madonna is mounted on the façade between them and, below, a beautiful entrance portal (1390) is decorated with scenes of Christ's passion. The interior's Gothic, Renaissance and Baroque features include Gothic sculptures of Calvary, a pewter font (1414) and a 15th-century Gothic pulpit. The Danish astronomer Tycho Brahe (1546–1601) is buried in a marble tomb here.

Kinský Palace 8
PALÁC KINSKÝCH

Map 3G. Staroměstské náměstí 12. Open Tue–Sun. Adm charge.

This stunning Rococo palace has a pretty pink and white stucco façade crowned with statues of the four elements by Ignaz Franz Platzer. It now houses the National Gallery's collection of prints and drawings and has an up-market restaurant.

Kinský arms on Golz-Kinský Palace

House at the Two Golden Bears [11]
DŮM U DVOU ZLATÝCH MEDVĚDŮ

Map 4F. Kožná 1. Closed to the public.

The present Renaissance building was constructed from two earlier houses in 1567. The ornate portal with reliefs of two bears, by court architect Bonifaz Wohlmut, is one of the most beautiful Renaissance portals in Prague. Magnificent arcades, also dating from the 16th century, have been preserved in the inner courtyard.

Church of St Nicholas [9]
KOSTEL SV. MIKULÁŠE

Map 3F. Staroměstské náměstí. Open daily and for evening concerts Apr–Nov. Free.

This stunning example of Baroque architecture, designed by Kilian Ignaz Dientzenhofer, dates from 1732. Its dramatic white façade is studded with statues by Antonín Braun. The magnificent dome has frescoes of the lives of St Nicholas and St Benedict by Kosmas Damian Asam. The interior is adorned by exquisite carvings, statues and frescoes by prominent artists, and in the nave there is a huge crown-shaped chandelier.

Carved Renaissance portal of the House at the Two Golden Bears

Church of St Gall [12]
KOSTEL SV. HAVLA

Map 4G. Havelská. Open for services: 12:15pm Mon–Fri, 8am Sun. Free.

In the 18th century this church, dating from around 1280, was given a Baroque facelift by Giovanni Santini-Aichel, who created a bold façade decorated with nine statues of saints. Rich interior furnishings include paintings by the Baroque artist Karel Škréta, who is buried here.

Old Town Hall [10]
STAROMĚSTSKÁ RADNICE

See pp14–15.

One of nine statues on the façade of St Gall's

OLD TOWN

Church of St Martin in the Wall ⓑ
KOSTEL SV. MARTINA VE ZDI

Map 4F. Martinská. Open for concerts. Free.

This 12th-century church became part of the newly erected town wall during the fortification of the Old Town in the 1200s. It was the first church where blessed wine, usually reserved for the clergy, was offered to the congregation. In 1787 the church was converted into a museum, but rebuilt in its original form in the 1900s.

Náprstek Museum ⓓ
NÁPRSTKOVO MUZEUM

Map 4F. Betlémské náměstí. Open Tue–Sun. Adm charge.

Vojta Náprstek, art patron and philanthropist, created this 19th-century museum as a tribute to modern industry. The fascinating collection now consists of artefacts from Asian and Native American cultures, with weapons, statues and masks from the Aztecs, Toltecs and Mayas.

Matthias Braun's statues on a portal of the Clam-Gallas Palace

Ceiling fresco by Václav Vavřinec Reiner in Church of St Giles

Church of St Giles ⓔ
KOSTEL SV. JILJÍ

Map 4F. Husova. Open for services daily. Free.

The inside of this church, founded in 1371, is essentially Baroque. The vaults have frescoes by Václav Vavřinec Reiner, who is buried here. The main fresco, a glorification of the Dominicans, shows St Dominic and his friars helping the pope defend the Catholic Church from non-believers.

Clam-Gallas Palace ⓕ
CLAM-GALLASŮV PALÁC

Map 3F. Husova 20. Open for concerts and temporary exhibitions only. Free.

The interior of this Baroque palace has been lovingly restored. The two pairs of Hercules, sculpted by Matthias Braun, on the grand portals give a taste of what lies within. The main staircase also has Braun statues, and is set off by a ceiling fresco, *The Triumph of Apollo* by Carlo Carlone.

Old Town Hall ❿
STAROMĚSTSKÁ RADNICE

One of the most striking buildings in Prague is the Old Town Hall, dating from 1338. Over the centuries it expanded and now comprises a row of colourful Gothic and Renaissance buildings. Its tower is 69.5 m (228 ft) high, and offers a spectacular view of the city.

The Gothic Main Door *leads to the Town Hall and Tower.*

The Old Town Coat of Arms *sits above the 1784 inscription, "Prague, Head of the Kingdom".*

Main entrance and tourist information

The Old Council Hall *has a well-preserved 16th-century ceiling.*

VISITORS' CHECKLIST

Map 3F. Staroměstské náměstí 1. Tel 724 508584.
Open daily. Adm charge.
www.prague-info.cz

OLD TOWN

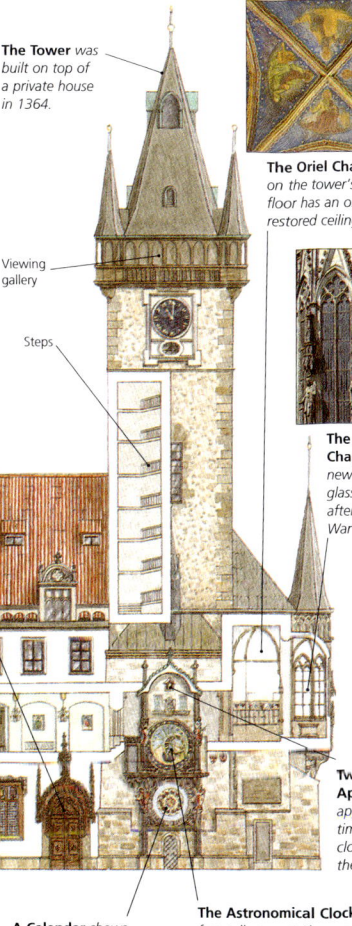

The Tower was built on top of a private house in 1364.

The Oriel Chapel on the tower's first floor has an ornate restored ceiling.

Viewing gallery

Steps

The Oriel Chapel had new stained-glass windows after World War II.

Twelve Apostles appear every time the clock strikes the hour.

A Calendar shows scenes of peasant life and pictures symbolizing months of the year.

The Astronomical Clock's face tells current time as well as relating the universe's planetary movements through the signs of the zodiac.

Mariánské Square ⑰
MARIÁNSKÉ NÁMĚSTÍ

Map 3F.

Two statues dominate the square from the corners of the forbidding Town Hall, built in 1912. One illustrates the story of long-lived Rabbi Löw *(see p23)* finally being caught by the Angel of Death. The other is the Iron Man, a local ghost condemned to roam the Old Town after murdering his mistress. A niche in the garden wall of the Clam-Gallas Palace houses a statue of the River Vltava, which is depicted as a nymph pouring water from a jug.

Charles Street ⑱
KARLOVA ULICE

Map 4F.

This 12th-century street was part of the Royal Route along which coronation processions passed on the way to Prague Castle. Many original Gothic and Renaissance houses remain, most converted into shops to attract tourists. Look out for At the Golden Well (No. 3), which has a magnificent Baroque façade and stucco reliefs of saints including St Roch and St Sebastian.

A 19th-century sign on the House at the Golden Snake in Charles St

Palace of the Lords of Kunštát ⑲
DŮM PÁNŮ Z KUNŠTÁTU

Map 4F. Řetězová. Open daily Apr–Oct. Adm charge.

Three of the best-preserved Romanesque rooms in Prague are found in the basement – originally the ground floor. The palace dates from 1200, but was enlarged in the Gothic style in the 15th century. It now houses a historical exhibition devoted to Bohemia's only Hussite king, George of Poděbrady.

Former Jesuit Church of the Holy Saviour in the Clementinum

Clementinum ⑳
KLEMENTINUM

Map 4F. Křižovnická 190, Mariánské náměstí 5, Karlova 1. Library open Mon–Sat. Church open only for services: 7pm Tue, 2pm, 8pm Sun. Guided tours 10am–4pm Mon. Free.

On its completion in 1726, the Clementinum was the largest building complex after Prague Castle. It has three churches, chapels, libraries, lecture halls, a courtyard and an observatory. Concerts are held in the beautiful Chapel of Mirrors.

OLD TOWN

Smetana Museum [21]
MUZEUM BEDŘICHA SMETANY

Map 4E. Novotného lávka 1.
Open Wed–Mon. Adm charge.

Sited by the river that inspired one of his most famous pieces – the Vltava – a former Neo-Renaissance waterworks has been turned into a memorial to Bedřich Smetana (1824–84), the father of Czech music.

Knights of the Cross Square [22]
KŘIŽOVNICKÉ NÁMĚSTÍ

Map 4E. Church of St Francis open only for services Sun–Fri. Gallery Křižovník open daily.

This small square in front of the Old Town Bridge Tower offers fine views across the Vltava. On the northern side is the Church of St Francis (Kostel sv. Františka). To the east is the Church of the Holy Saviour, part of the Clementinum complex, and on the western side is the Gallery Křižovníků. In the square stands a large bronze Neo-Gothic statue of Charles IV.

Statue of Charles IV (1848) in Knights of the Cross Square

STREET LIFE

RESTAURANTS

U vejvodů
Map 4E. Jilská 4. Tel 224 219999.
Cheap
A convenient place open every day from 10am until 2am.

Bellevue
Map 4E. Smetanovo nábřeží 18. Tel 222 221443.
Expensive
Formal continental dining.

CAFÉS

Ebel Coffeehouse
Map 3G. Templová 7.
You won't find a better cup of coffee in the city.

Grand Café
Map 3G. Staroměstské náměstí 22. Tel 221 632522.
A civilized way to watch the Old Town Hall's clock go through its hourly paces.

See p80 for price codes.

Slavia
Map 4E. Smetanovo nábřeží 2.
Tel 224 218493.
The café with the best view of the castle and Charles Bridge.

SHOPPING

Blue
Map 3F. Malé náměstí 14.
A different kind of glass shop with modern, fun designs.

U rytíře Kryštofa
Map 4G. Kožná 8.
A weird treasure trove of goodies, from battle-axes to chastity belts.

Arzenal
Map 3F. Valentinská 11.
A wide range of exquisite glass and crystal is sold here.

Palladium
Map 3H. Náměstí Republiky 1.
A mall built on the site of a former army barracks.

JEWISH QUARTER
JOSEFOV

Though the old ghetto was razed in the 19th century, much of the area's fascinating history is preserved in the synagogues around the Old Jewish Cemetery, while the newer streets, such as Pařížská, are lined with many delightful Art Nouveau buildings. The old lanes to the east of the former ghetto lead to the quiet haven of St Agnes Convent, restored as a branch of the National Gallery.

SIGHTS AT A GLANCE

Synagogues and Churches
Pinkas Synagogue ❹
Klausen Synagogue ❺
Old-New Synagogue pp24–5 ❻
High Synagogue ❼
Maisel Synagogue ❾
Church of the Holy Ghost ❿
Spanish Synagogue ⓫
Church of St Simon and St Jude ⓭
Church of St Castullus ⓮

Concert Hall
Rudolfinum ❶

Museums and Galleries
Museum of Decorative Arts ❷
St Agnes of Bohemia Convent ⓯

Historic Buildings
Jewish Town Hall ❽
Cubist Houses ⓬

Cemeteries
Old Jewish Cemetery pp22–3 ❸

SEE ALSO

• *Street Life p27*

◀ *Densely packed gravestones in the Old Jewish Cemetery*

Stage of the Dvořák Hall in the Rudolfinum

Rudolfinum ❶

Map 3F. Alšovo nábřeží 12. Open Tue–Sun. Adm charge for exhibits.

Home of the Czech Philharmonic Orchestra, the Rudolfinum is an impressive landmark on the river Vltava. This outstanding example of Czech Neo-Renaissance style houses concert halls and modern art exhibits. Its curving balustrade is decorated with statues of distinguished Czech, Austrian and German composers and artists.

Museum of Decorative Arts ❷
UMĚLECKOPRŮMYSLOVÉ MUZEUM

Map 3F. 17. listopadu 2. Open Tue–Sun. Adm charge.

This French Neo-Renaissance style museum houses one of the world's largest glass collections. Many fine pieces of Bohemian, Medieval and Venetian Renaissance glass, as well as Meissen porcelain, the Gobelin tapestries, fashion, textiles, printing, photography and furniture are on display. The extensive art library houses over 170,000 publications.

Old Jewish Cemetery ❸
STARÝ ŽIDOVSKÝ HŘBITOV

See pp22–3.

Pinkas Synagogue ❹
PINKASOVA SYNAGÓGA

Map 3F. Široká 3. Open Sun–Fri. Adm charge.

The second-oldest synagogue in Prague (1535), its core is a hall with Gothic vaulting. A memorial to the Jewish-Czech citizens held at Terezín concentration camp and later deported to other Nazi extermination camps, it has the names of the 77,297 who did not return inscribed on its walls. The building also houses an exhibition of children's drawings from Terezín.

Names of Holocaust victims on Pinkas Synagogue wall

Klausen Synagogue ❺
KLAUSOVÁ SYNAGÓGA

Map 3F. U starého hřbitova 3a. Open Sun–Fri. Adm charge.

This High Baroque structure (1694), with its fine barrel-vaulted interior and rich stucco decorations, houses Hebrew prints and manuscripts and an exhibition of Jewish festivals and traditions. Adjoining is a tiny medieval castle-style building erected as the ceremonial hall of the Jewish Burial Society.

JEWISH QUARTER

Old-New Synagogue ⑥
STARONOVÁ SYNAGÓGA

See pp24–5.

Torah shield, High Synagogue

High Synagogue ⑦
VYSOKÁ SYNAGÓGA

Map 3F. Červená 4. Open for services only.

Constructed in 1568 with funds from its rich mayor Mordechai Maisel, the High Synagogue was built in elegant Renaissance fashion. Its name is believed to derive from the fact that the prayer room is located upstairs. Additions and reconstructions have been carried out over the years, but the synagogue's interior retains its original vaulting and stucco decoration.

Jewish Town Hall ⑧
ŽIDOVSKÁ RADNICE

Map 3F. Maiselova 18. Closed to the public.

The hands of the town hall's Rococo clock turn backwards, as the Hebrew letters on its face are read from right to left. A gift from Mordechai Maisel in the 1570s, this attractive building was renovated in 1763–5 in a flowery Late Baroque style.

Maisel Synagogue ⑨
MAISELOVA SYNAGÓGA

Map 3F. Maiselova 10. Open Sun–Fri. Adm charge.

Built as a private synagogue for Mayor Maisel in 1591, it was destroyed by the ghetto fire of 1689. Its present crenellated, Neo-Gothic style, dating from the early 1900s, houses an exhibition on the history of Jews in the Czech lands from the Middle Ages to the 18th century.

Church of the Holy Ghost ⑩
KOSTEL SV. DUCHA

Map 3F. Dušní, Široká. Open only for services. Free.

Built in the mid-1300s, the exterior of this single-naved church, rebuilt after the 1689 ghetto fire, preserves the original Gothic buttresses and high windows, but the vault of the nave was rebuilt in Baroque style. Inside is a painting of St Joseph on the high altar (1760), a 14th-century Pietà and busts of St Wenceslas and St Adalbert.

Façade and clock tower of the Jewish Town Hall

Old Jewish Cemetery ❸
STARÝ ŽIDOVSKÝ HŘBITOV

This remarkable site, founded in 1478, is a moving memorial to Prague's once sizable Jewish community. Due to lack of space, people were buried up to 12 layers deep. Today, over 12,000 gravestones are crammed into the tiny area, but over 100,000 people may be buried here.

David Gans, the writer-astronomer, has a tombstone decorated with symbols of his name – a star of David and a goose (Gans in German).

The Pinkas Synagogue is the second-oldest in Prague.

Main entrance

The Oldest Tomb is that of the writer Rabbi Avigdor Kara (1439).

The Gravestone of Moses Beck, the last person to be buried here, in 1787.

Klausen Synagogue

The Nephele Mound was the burial place of infants under a year old.

Fragments Embedded in the Wall are from 14th-century Gothic tombstones brought here from an older Jewish cemetery.

JEWISH QUARTER

23

The Prague Burial Society, founded in 1564, carried out ritual burials and performed charitable works.

Rabbi Löw's Tombstone is the most visited grave in the cemetery.

Museum of Decorative Arts

Neo-Romanesque Ceremonial Hall

Mordechai Maisel (1528–1601) was the philanthropic Mayor of Prague's Jewish Town.

VISITORS' CHECKLIST

Map 3F. Široká 3 (main entrance). Tel 222 317191 (bookings), 222 749211 (Jewish Museum). Open Sun–Fri. Adm charge.
www.jewishmuseum.cz

Hendela Bassevi's Grave is decorated with this elaborate tombstone.

Old-New Synagogue
STARONOVÁ SYNAGOGA

Built around 1270, this is Europe's oldest synagogue and one of Prague's earliest Gothic buildings. Today it is still the religious centre for Prague's Jews. Originally it was called the New Synagogue until another synagogue was built nearby, but this was later destroyed.

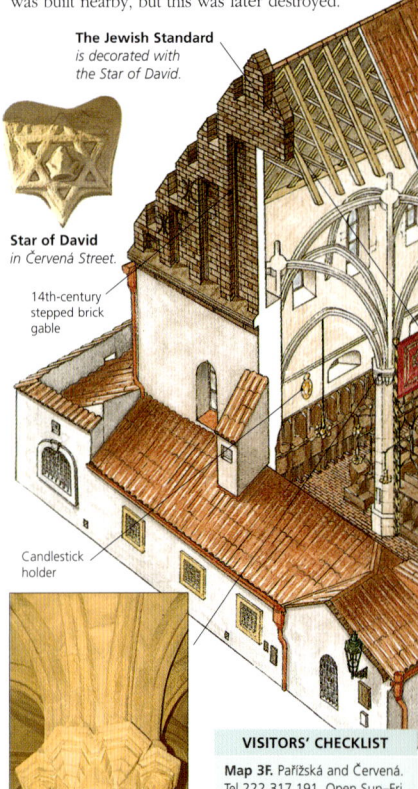

The Jewish Standard *is decorated with the Star of David.*

Star of David *in Červená Street.*

14th-century stepped brick gable

Candlestick holder

Five-rib Vaulting, decorated with vine leaves and ivy, is supported by octagonal pillars.

VISITORS' CHECKLIST

Map **3F**. Pařížská and Červená.
Tel 222 317 191. Open Sun–Fri.
Closed Jewish holidays.
Adm charge.
www.synagogue.cz

JEWISH QUARTER

The Ark *is the holiest place in the synagogue and holds the sacred Torah scrolls.*

Rabbi Löw's Chair, *where the distinguished 16th-century scholar and Chief Rabbi sat.*

The Right-hand Nave *has 12 narrow windows evoking the 12 tribes of Israel.*

Wrought-iron Gothic grille surrounding cantor's platform and lectern

Entrance from Červená Street

The Decorated Tympanum *above the door in the south vestibule.*

Motif of the Ten Commandments on the Spanish Synagogue's façade

Spanish Synagogue ⑪
ŠPANĚLSKÁ SYNAGÓGA

Map 3F. Vězeňská 1.
Open Sun–Fri. Adm charge.

The newest synagogue in this part of Prague, it was built in flamboyant pseudo-Moorish style in 1868, replacing Prague's oldest synagogue, the Old School (Stará škola). The arabesques and stucco decorations are reminiscent of Spain's Alhambra. It houses an exhibition on the history of Jews in Bohemia and Moravia.

Cubist Houses ⑫
KUBISTICKÉ DOMY

Map 2F. Elišky Krásnohorské, 10–14. Closed to the public.

Rebuilding the old Jewish Quarter around 1900 gave

Cubist-style atlantes framing a window in Elišky Krásnohorské Street

Prague's architects scope to experiment with many new styles. Most buildings are covered with flowing Art Nouveau decoration, but at Bílkova and Elišky Krásnohorské a Cubist avant-garde example shows a plain façade with repeated geometrical shapes.

Church of St Simon and St Jude ⑬
KOSTEL SV. ŠIMONA A JUDY

Map 2F. U milosrdných.
Open for concerts. Free.

The Bohemia Brethren built this church with high Late Gothic windows in 1615–20. In the 1700s it became Prague's first anatomy lecture hall, and the complex still serves as a hospital – the Na Františku. The church now hosts concerts.

Detail of Baroque façade of Church of St Simon and St Jude

Church of St Castullus ⑭
KOSTEL SV. HAŠTALA

Map 2G. Haštalské náměstí.
Opens irregularly. Free.

One of the finest Gothic buildings in Prague, the church was erected in the late 1300s. On

JEWISH QUARTER

the north side the double nave, with its beautiful slender pillars supporting a delicate ribbed vault, survived the 1689 fire. Inside there are wall paintings (c.1375) in the sacristy, Baroque furnishings and a decorated metal font (c.1550).

St Agnes of Bohemia Convent ⓯
KLÁŠTER SV. ANEŽKY ČESKÉ

Map 2G. Anežská 12. Open Tue–Sun. Adm charge.

In around 1231 Agnes, sister of King Wenceslas I, founded a convent of the Poor Clares. One of Bohemia's first Gothic buildings, it was fully restored in the 1960s. The National Gallery now uses it to exhibit medieval and Renaissance art.

One of the 14th-century altarpieces in St Agnes Convent

STREET LIFE

RESTAURANTS

King Solomon
Map 3F. Široká 8.
Tel 224 818752.
Moderate
Prague's foremost kosher restaurant.

Barock
Map 2F. Pařížská 24.
Tel 222 329221.
Expensive
Perennially fashionable restaurant.

BARS AND CAFÉS

Alcohol Bar
Map 3F. Dušní 6.
A cool and relaxed place to enjoy a drink.

Café Franz Kafka
Map 3F. Široká 12.
Take time out for café Vienna and apple strudel.

See p80 for price codes.

SHOPPING

Spanish Synagogue Gift Shop
Map 2F. Vězeňská 1.
Exquisite Torah pointers, skull caps and other unique gifts, such as a watch in the style of the clock on the Jewish Town Hall (see p21).

Antique Cinotler
Map 3F. Maiselova 9.
Specializes in antique jewellery and precious stones, but also stocks an interesting selection of fine art, glass, porcelain, clocks, watches and decorative items.

Antique Kaprova
Map 3F. Kaprova 12.
Serious collector's shop specializing in prints and small decorative items such as clocks and lamps. If you can't find what you want, just ask and they'll point you in the right direction.

PRAGUE CASTLE AND HRADČANY
PRAŽSKÝ HRAD A HRADČANY

Founded in the 9th century by Prince Bořivoj, Prague Castle and the Gothic spires of its attendant cathedral, St Vitus's, tower above the city from the long hill known as Hradčany. After a fire in 1541, the badly damaged buildings of the Castle complex were rebuilt. The area abounds with sites of interest to art and history lovers, as well as romantic hidden paths and parks.

SIGHTS AT A GLANCE

Churches and Monasteries
St Vitus's Cathedral pp32–3 ③
St George's Basilica ⑥
Capuchin Monastery ⑳
The Loreto pp36–7 ㉑
Strahov Monastery pp40–41 ㉔

Palaces
Royal Palace ⑤
Lobkowicz Palace ⑨
Belvedere ⑫
Archbishop's Palace ⑮
Martinic Palace ⑰
Černín Palace ㉒

Historic Buildings
Prague Castle ①
Powder Tower ④
Dalibor Tower ⑩

Museums and Galleries
Picture Gallery of Prague Castle ②
St George's Convent ⑦
Riding School ⑭
Sternberg Palace ⑯
Schwarzenberg Palace ⑱

Historic Streets
Golden Lane ⑧
New World ⑲
Pohořelec ㉓

Parks and Gardens
South Gardens ⑪
Royal Garden ⑬

SEE ALSO
- Street Life p43

KEY
- Ⓜ Metro station
- Tram stop
- ℹ Tourist information

◀ The main entrance to Prague Castle

Prague Castle ❶
PRAŽSKÝ HRAD

Map 2C. Open daily.
Adm charge.

Despite fires and invasions, this impressive castle has retained churches, chapels, halls and towers from every period of its history, from its Gothic cathedral to Renaissance additions and Late Baroque and Neo-Classical courtyards. Its sights include St Vitus's Cathedral, St George's Basilica, the Royal Palace and Golden Lane.

Picture Gallery of Prague Castle ❷
OBRAZÁRNA PRAŽSKÉHO HRADU

Map 2C. Prague Castle, second courtyard. Open daily. Adm charge.

The gallery holds works of art collected since the reign of Rudolph II. Paintings from the 16th to the 18th centuries form the bulk of the collection, but there are also sculptures. Highlights include Titian's *The Toilet of a Young Lady*, Rubens' *The Assembly of the Olympic Gods* and Guido Reni's *The Centaur Nessus Abducting Deianeira*.

St Vitus's Cathedral ❸
CHRÁM SV. VÍTA

See pp32–3.

Powder Tower ❹
PRAŠNÁ VĚŽ

Map 2C. Prague Castle, Vikářská. Open daily. Adm charge.

A tower was built here in the late 15th century by King Vladislav as a cannon bastion overlooking the Stag Moat. The tower was rebuilt after the fire of 1541 for the gunsmith

View of the Powder Tower from across the Stag Moat

and bell founder Thomas Jaroš, and later uses included a laboratory for alchemists. In the 1960s it became a museum with exhibits relating to Jaroš and alchemy.

Royal Palace ❺
KRÁLOVSKÝ PALÁC

Map 2C. Prague Castle, third courtyard. Open daily.
Adm charge.

From the 11th century the Royal Palace was the seat of Bohemian princes. The building has three different layers. A Romanesque palace (c.1165) forms the cellars of the present building. Above this two more palaces were added between the 13th and 14th centuries. In 1502 the final layer – the massive Gothic Vladislav Hall with its rib vaulting – was finished. In 1924 the Palace underwent extensive renovation.

Façade and towers of St George's Basilica

St George's Basilica ❻
BAZILIKA SV. JIŘÍ

Map 2C. Jiřské náměstí. Open daily. Adm charge.

Founded by Prince Vratislav in around 920, this is Prague's best-preserved Romanesque church. The restored twin towers and austere interior give a good idea of the church's original appearance, but the red façade was an 18th century Baroque addition.

St George's Convent ❼
KLÁŠTER SV. JIŘÍ

Map 2C. Prague Castle, Jiřské náměstí. Open daily. Adm charge.

The first convent in Bohemia was founded here close to the Royal Palace in 973 by Prince Boleslav II, whose sister Mlada was its first abbess. The Romanesque building houses artworks from the National Gallery. On the lower floor are 14th century paintings and sculpture, represented by many naive woodcarvings and panel paintings. Later Gothic art is on the ground floor, while the first floor houses the Renaissance and Baroque collections, with dramatic biblical paintings and statues of saints and angels in flamboyant poses.

Golden Lane ❽
ZLATÁ ULIČKA

Map 2D. Adm charge.

Named after the goldmiths who lived here in the 1600s, this short, narrow street is one of Prague's most picturesque. Tiny, brightly painted houses, built into the Castle walls, date from the late 1500s. Writer Franz Kafka lived at No. 22.

One of the tiny houses in Prague's picturesque Golden Lane

St Vitus's Cathedral ❸
KATEDRÁLA SV. VÍTA, VÁCLAVA A VOJTĚCHA

This spectacular Gothic cathedral dominates the city from its position on Hradčany Hill. A walk around St Vitus's takes you back through almost 800 years of history. Work began on the building in 1344 but it was not completed until 1929. Today, it houses the crown jewels and the tomb of "Good King" Wenceslas.

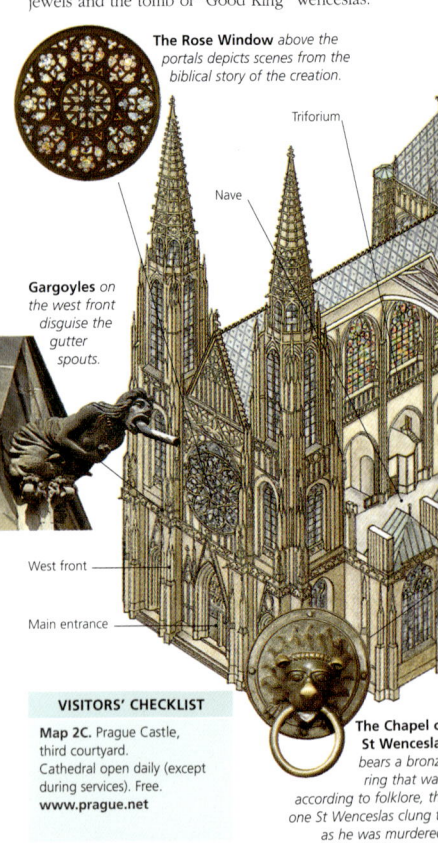

The Rose Window above the portals depicts scenes from the biblical story of the creation.

Triforium

Nave

Gargoyles on the west front disguise the gutter spouts.

West front

Main entrance

VISITORS' CHECKLIST

Map 2C. Prague Castle, third courtyard.
Cathedral open daily (except during services). Free.
www.prague.net

The Chapel of St Wenceslas bears a bronze ring that was, according to folklore, the one St Wenceslas clung to as he was murdered.

PRAGUE CASTLE AND HRADČANY | 33

Slender Flying Buttresses surround the exterior of the nave and chancel.

Baroque bell tower

Chancel

To Royal Palace

The tomb of St Wenceslas

Gothic Vaulting supports the three Gothic arches of the Golden Portal.

The Golden Portal was built as a festival entrance in around 1373–4. Above it is a mosaic of The Last Judgment.

Lobkowicz Palace 9
LOBKOVICKÝ PALÁC

Map 2D. Jiřská 3. Open daily; Toy Museum Tue–Sun. Adm charge.

This is one of the palaces that sprang up after the fire of 1541, when Hradčany was almost totally destroyed. Dating from the mid-16th century, some original *sgraffito* on the façade has been preserved, but most of the palace is of 17th-century reconstruction. The banqueting hall is adorned with mythological frescoes. There are magnificent views across Prague from the terrace restaurant. Opposite at No. 6 is a delightful museum of toys with exhibits from ancient Greece to the present.

Detail of 16th-century sgraffito on the façade of Lobkowicz Palace

Dalibor Tower 10
DALIBORKA

Map 2D. Prague Castle, Zlatá ulička. Open daily. Adm charge.

This 15th-century tower with a conical roof was part of the fortifications built by Vladislav Jagiello, whose coat of arms adorn the outer wall. The tower, named after its first inmate, Dalibor of Kozojedy, was a prison until 1781. While awaiting execution, Dalibor was kept in an underground dungeon. According to legend, people came to listen to him playing his violin and lowered food and drink to him. Bedřich Smetana used the story in his opera *Dalibor*.

Allipandi's music pavilion in the South Gardens

South Gardens 11
JIŽNÍ ZAHRADY

Map 3C. Prague Castle (access from Hradčanské náměstí). Open daily Apr–Oct. Free.

Occupying the long, narrow band of land below the Castle, South Gardens comprise several small gardens linked together: the Paradise Garden (Rajská zahrada) of 1562 has a circular pavilion, the 19th-century Garden on the Ramparts (Zahrada Na valech) has two obelisks, and the former Hartig Garden, designed in the 1960s, has a music pavilion.

Old prison in the Dalibor Tower

The Belvedere, Emperor Ferdinand I's summer palace in the Royal Garden beside Prague Castle

Belvedere ⑫
BELVEDÉR

Map 2D. Prague Castle, Royal Garden. Closed for reconstruction.

Built between 1538 and 1560, this is one of the finest Italian Renaissance buildings north of the Alps. Also called the Royal Summer Palace (Královský letohrádek), the Belvedere is an arcaded summerhouse with Ionic columns topped by a roof shaped like an inverted ship's hull. There are also ornate reliefs inside the arcade. In the garden in front of the palace stands the Singing Fountain (1568), which owes its name to the musical sound the water makes as it hits the bronze bowl. The Belvedere is now an art gallery, but is currently closed for renovations.

Royal Garden ⑬
KRÁLOVSKÁ ZAHRADA

Map 2C. Prague Castle, U Prašného mostu. Open daily May–Oct. Free.

The garden was created in 1534 for Ferdinand I. Its appearance has been altered over time, but some examples of 16th-century garden architecture have survived, notably the Belvedere and the Ball Game Hall (Míčovna), built in 1569. The Hall is covered in beautiful, though much restored, Renaissance *sgraffito*, a form of decoration created by cutting a design through the wet top layer of plaster on to a contrasting undercoat. The garden is a beautiful place to stroll, especially in spring when thousands of tulips bloom in its immaculate beds. This is the place where tulips were first acclimatized to Europe.

Antonin Braun's statue of The Allegory of Night in front of the sgraffito decoration of the Ball Game Hall in the Royal Garden

36 | PRAGUE AREA BY AREA

The Loreto ㉑
LORETA

The Loreto has been an important place of pilgrimage since 1626. At the heart of this elaborate shrine is the Santa Casa – a copy of the house where it is believed the Virgin Mary received the Incarnation.

The Baroque Front Entrance *is adorned with statues of St Joseph and St John the Baptist.*

Chapel of St Joseph

Fountain

The Loreto Treasury *contains valuable items, like this gold-plated, diamond-encrusted monstrance.*

Entrance from Loretánské náměstí

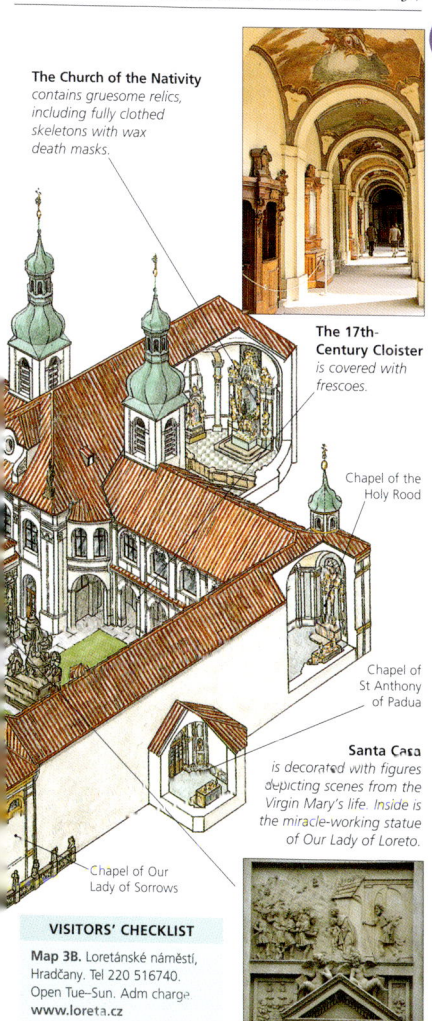

PRAGUE CASTLE AND HRADČANY 37

The Church of the Nativity
contains gruesome relics, including fully clothed skeletons with wax death masks.

The 17th-Century Cloister *is covered with frescoes.*

Chapel of the Holy Rood

Chapel of St Anthony of Padua

Santa Casa *is decorated with figures depicting scenes from the Virgin Mary's life. Inside is the miracle-working statue of Our Lady of Loreto.*

Chapel of Our Lady of Sorrows

VISITORS' CHECKLIST

Map 3B. Loretánské náměstí, Hradčany. Tel 220 516740. Open Tue–Sun. Adm charge.
www.loreta.cz

Přichovský coat of arms at the Archbishop's Palace

Riding School ⑭
JÍZDÁRNA

Map 2C. Prague Castle. Open during exhibitions. Adm charge.

The 17th-century Riding School forms one side of U Prašného mostu, a road running along the northern side of Prague Castle. In the mid-20th century it was converted into an exhibition hall, which now holds important exhibitions of painting and sculpture. A garden provides great views of St Vitus's Cathedral and the castle's fortifications.

Archbishop's Palace ⑮
ARCIBISKUPSKÝ PALÁC

Map 3C. Hradčanské náměstí 16. Not open to the public.

In 1562, Ferdinand I bought the palace for his Catholic Archbishop. Originally a Renaissance structure, in the 1760s this palace was given a spectacular cream-coloured Rococo façade which was designed by Johann Joseph Wirch for Archbishop Antonín Příchovský, whose coat of arms sits proudly above the portal.

Sternberg Palace ⑯
ŠTERNBERSKÝ PALÁC

Map 2B. Hradčanské náměstí 15. Open Tue–Sun. Adm charge.

This fine Baroque building has been used since 1946 to house the National Gallery's collection of European art, arranged on three floors around the central courtyard of the palace.

The façade of the Riding School at Prague Castle

PRAGUE CASTLE AND HRADČANY

The Carmelite monastery next to the Schwarzenberg Palace

Among the notable paintings that date from the 14th century are *Adam and Eve* by Lucas Cranach the Elder, *Head of Christ* by El Greco, *Haymaking* by Pieter Brueghel the Elder, and Picasso's *Self-Portrait*.

Martinic Palace ⓱
MARTINICKÝ PALÁC

Map 3B. Hradčanské náměstí 8. Open daily. Adm charge.

Dating from 1563, this was the first example of late Renaissance building in Prague. When the palace was being restored in the 1960s–70s, workmen discovered the original 16th-century façade, decorated with ornate *sgraffito*, depicting Old Testament scenes, more was discovered in the courtyard.

Schwarzenberg Palace ⓲
SCHWARZENBERSKÝ PALÁC

Map 3C. Hradčanské náměstí 2. Open Tue–Sun. Adm charge.

From a distance, the façade of this exquisite Renaissance palace appears to be clad in projecting pyramid-shaped stonework, but it is an illusion created by black and white *sgraffito* patterns incised on a flat wall. Built by Italian architect Agostino Galli in 1545–76, the gabled palace is Florentine rather than Bohemian in style. Inside, four painted ceilings on the second floor date from 1580. The renovated palace is now the permanent setting for the Renaissance collections of the National Gallery.

New World ⓳
NOVÝ SVĚT

Map 2B.

Now a charming street of small cottages, Nový Svět (New World) was the former name for this area of Hradčany. Developed in the mid-1300s for castle workers, the area was twice destroyed by fire, so most cottages date from the 1600s. To defy their poverty, residents chose golden house signs for their modest homes – such as a Golden Pear, a Grape, a Bush or an Acorn.

Strahov Monastery 24
STRAHOVSKÝ KLÁŠTER

Dating from 1140, Strahov Monastery has retained its Romanesque core in spite of fires, wars and extensive renovation. After a fire in 1258, it was rebuilt in the Gothic style, with Baroque additions. Its library in the Philosophical and Theological halls is over 800 years old.

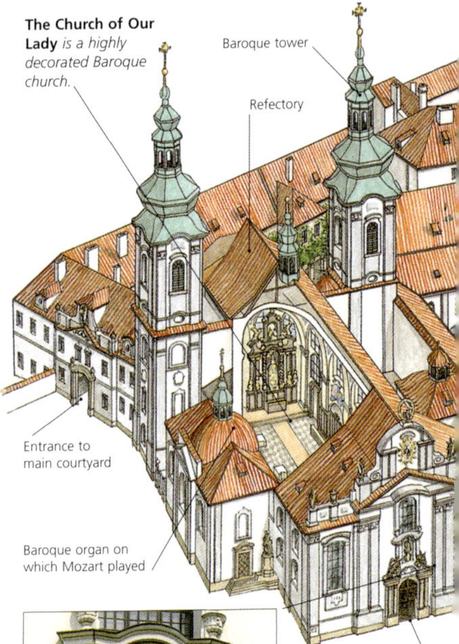

The Church of Our Lady *is a highly decorated Baroque church.*

Baroque tower

Refectory

Entrance to main courtyard

Baroque organ on which Mozart played

Entrance to Church of Our Lady

Elaborate Statues *were added to the western façade in the 1750s.*

PRAGUE CASTLE AND HRADČANY | 41

A Statue of St John *the evangelist stands in the Theological Hall.*

A Ceiling Fresco *in the Philosophical Hall, built in 1782 to hold the Baroque bookcases and their valuable books, depicts the Struggle of Mankind to Know Real History by Franz Maulbertsch.*

Convent and art gallery

The bust of Joseph II *over the entrance gate.*

Entrance to libraries

Decorated façade of the Philosophical Hall

The Theological Hall's Treasures include a 17th-century astronomical globe and a facsimile of a precious 9th-century gospel book.

VISITORS' CHECKLIST

Map 4A. Královská Kanonie Premonstrátů na Strahově. Strahovské nádvoří 1. Tel 233 107711. Open daily except Easter Sun, 25 Dec. Adm charge.
www.strahovmonastery.cz

Church of the Capuchin Monastery

Capuchin Monastery 20
KAPUCÍNSKÝ KLÁŠTER

Map 3B. Loretánské náměstí 6. Closed to the public except the church. Free.

Bohemia's first Capuchin monastery was founded here in 1600. Next to it is the Church of Our Lady Queen of Angels, a single-naved building with plain furnishings, typical of the ascetic Capuchin order. The church is famous for its miraculous statue of the Madonna and Child and its nativity scenes.

The Loreto 21
LORETA

See pp36–7.

Černín Palace 22
ČERNÍNSKÝ PALÁC

Map 3B. Loretánské náměstí 5. Closed to the public.

Built during the 17th and 18th centuries, the palace is 150 m (500 ft) long with a row of 30 massive Corinthian half-columns running the length of its upper storeys. One of Prague's most monumental buildings, in 1918 it was restored to its original design. A few days after the Communist Coup in 1948 the Foreign Minister, Jan Masaryk, the son of Czechoslovakia's first President, Tomáš Masaryk, died as the result of a fall from a Palace window. He was the only non-Communist in the government that had just been formed. No-one really knows whether he was pushed or jumped, but he is still widely mourned. The Palace towers over an attractive, grassy square.

Capital on Černín Palace

Pohořelec 23

Map 3A.

First settled in 1375, this is one of the oldest parts of Prague,

Kučera Palace, a Rococo building in Pohořelec

PRAGUE CASTLE AND HRADČANY

but the name is of more recent origin: Pohořelec means "place destroyed by fire". Three times this has occurred, the last time in 1741. Pohořelec is now a large open square on a hill high over the city and part of the main access route to Prague Castle. In the centre stands a monument to St John Nepomuk (1752). The houses around the square are mainly Baroque and Rococo.

Strahov Monastery 24
STRAHOVSKÝ KLÁŠTER

See pp40–41.

STREET LIFE

RESTAURANTS

U ševce Matouše
Map 2B. Loretánské náměstí 4.
Tel 220 514536.
Moderate
"At the Cobbler Matouš" makes an art of melting cheese on beefsteaks.

Lví dvůr
Map 2C. U Prašného mostu 6.
Tel 224 372361.
Expensive
Rooftop dining room gives fabulous views of St Vitus. Sublime suckling pig.

U Zlaté hrušky
Map 2B. Nový Svět 3.
Tel 220 941244.
Expensive
"At the Golden Pear" serves delicious game dishes in a picturesque setting.

Restaurant u Lorety
Map 3B. Loretánské náměstí 8.
Tel 220 517369.
Moderate
Meat-and-potatoes dining with sweeping views. Very steep staircase.

Cowboys
Map 3C. Nerudova 40.
Tel 296 826107.
Expensive
Marvellous views from the rooftop terrace. Italian and Mediterranean specialities.

PUBS AND CAFÉS

U Černého vola
Map 3A. Loretánské náměstí 1.
Part of the proceeds from the pub "At the Black Ox" go to the nearby school for the blind. Watch the regulars knock back litre after litre of beer.

U Zavěšenýho Kafe
Map 3B. Úvoz 6.
Rustic "The Hanging Coffee" is named after the practice of paying for an extra cup for whoever wanders in next.

Na Baště
Map 2C. Zahrada na Baště, Prague Castle.
Out-of-the-way, peaceful restaurant-café in the castle's Garden on the Bastion.

Kajetánka
Map 2C. Hradčanske náměstí 1.
Sip espresso on the rooftop while peering through the telescope at the city below. Lunch on the quiet patio.

SHOPPING

Hračky
Map 3B. Loretánské Náměstí 3.
An enchanting and colourful selection of traditional Czech toys.

See p80 for price codes.

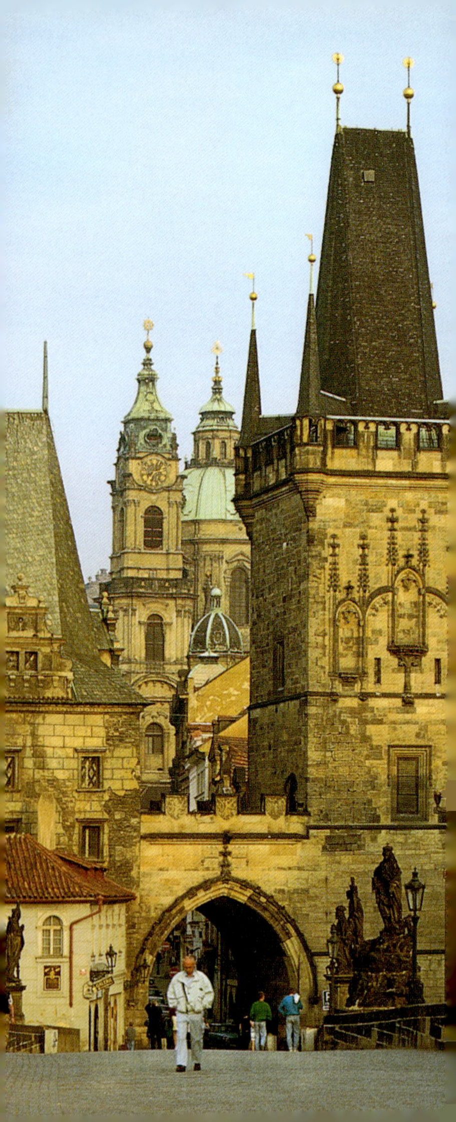

PRAGUE AREA BY AREA

LITTLE QUARTER
MALÁ STRANA

Founded in 1257, the Little Quarter is rich in splendid Baroque palaces and old houses with attractive signs. Built on the slopes below the Castle hill, there are superb views across the river to the Old Town.

SIGHTS AT A GLANCE

Churches
Church of St Thomas ③
Church of St Nicholas pp48–9 ⑤
Church of Our Lady Victorious ⑨
Church of Our Lady beneath the Chain ⑬
Church of St Lawrence ㉒

Parks and Gardens
Vrtba Garden ⑧
Vojan Park ⑰
Ledebour Garden ⑲
Observation Tower ⑳
Mirror Maze ㉑
Observatory ㉓
Petřín Park ㉕
Funicular Railway ㉖

Museums
Kampa Museum of Modern Art ⑱
Museum of Music ㉗

Historic Monuments
Hunger Wall ㉔

Historic Restaurants and Beer Halls
At St Thomas's ②
At the Three Ostriches ⑮

Historic Streets and Squares
Little Quarter Square ④
Nerudova Street ⑥
Italian Street ⑦
Maltese Square ⑩
Grand Priory Square ⑫
Bridge Street ⑯

Bridges and Islands
Kampa Island ⑪
Charles Bridge pp54–7 ⑭

Palaces
Wallenstein Palace and Garden ①
Michna Palace ㉘

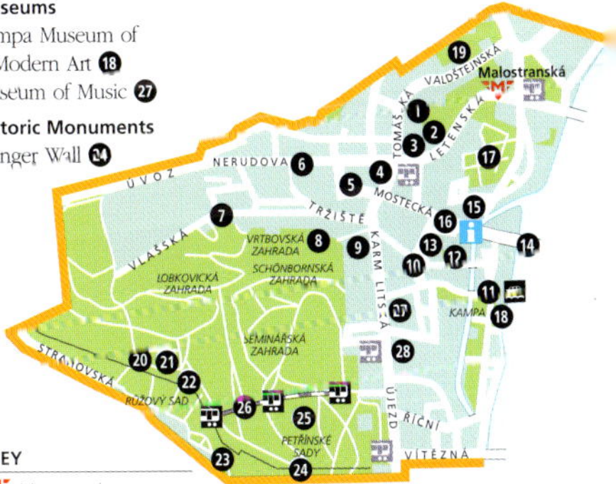

KEY

- Metro station
- Tram stop
- Funicular railway
- River boat boarding point
- Tourist information

0 metres 250
0 yards 250

SEE ALSO

- *Street Life p59*

◁ Charles Bridge and the Little Quarter Bridge Towers

The main hall of Wallenstein Palace

Wallenstein Palace and Garden ❶
VALDŠTEJNSKÝ PALÁC

Map 3D. Valdštejnské náměstí 4. Palace open Sat & Sun. Riding School open Tue–Sun. Garden open daily Apr–Oct. Free.

Completed in 1630, this vast Baroque palace was built as a monument by Count Albrecht von Wallenstein (1583–1634) to himself. The magnificent main hall has a ceiling fresco of Wallenstein portrayed as Mars. The gardens are laid out in Renaissance style. A huge pavilion looks out over a fountain and rows of bronze statues, and another pavilion has frescoes with scenes of the Argonauts and the Golden Fleece. There is also a large ornamental pond. The palace now houses the Czech senate.

At St Thomas's ❷
U SV. TOMÁŠE

Map 3D. Letenská 12. Open daily.

At St Thomas's, the oldest beer hall in Prague, features 17th-century stalactites and stalagmites. It is now part of the Brewery Bar of The Augustine, a boutique hotel. Augustinian monks first brewed beer here in 1352. The brewery was appointed sole purveyor of beer to Prague Castle, until 1951.

Church of St Thomas ❸
KOSTEL SV. TOMÁŠE

Map 3D. Josefská 8. Open for services daily. Free.

After a lightning strike in 1723, the original Gothic church (1379) was rebuilt, its shape preserved in the dramatic

Baroque ceiling in the nave of the Church of St Thomas

LITTLE QUARTER

Baroque façade. Little remains of its Gothic origins apart from the spire. The skeleton of martyr St Just rests in a glass coffin below a Crucifixion by Antonín Stevens, one of several superb works of religious art in this church.

Little Quarter Square ❹
MALOSTRANSKÉ NÁMĚSTÍ

Map 3D.

The square has been the centre of the Little Quarter since 1257. Most houses around the square have a medieval core, but all were rebuilt in the Renaissance and Baroque periods. The Baroque church of St Nicholas dominates the square. Along its upper side runs the vast Neo-Classical façade of Lichtenstein Palace. Other important buildings include the Little Quarter Town Hall with its Renaissance façade, the Sternberg Palace and the Smiřický Palace, whose turrets and hexagonal towers make it an unmistakable landmark. The Baroque Kaiserstein Palace is situated at the eastern side.

Arcade in front of buildings on the north side of Little Quarter Square

Church of St Nicholas ❺
KOSTEL SV. MIKULÁŠE

See pp48–9.

Sign of Jan Neruda's house, At the Two Suns, 47 Nerudova Street

Nerudova Street ❻
NERUDOVA ULICE

Map 3C.

A picturesque narrow street leading up to Prague Castle, Nerudova is named after the Czech poet Jan Neruda, who lived at the house called At the Two Suns (No. 47). Until 1770, Prague's houses were distinguished by heraldic signs. Look out for the Red Eagle (No. 6), the Golden Horseshoe (No. 34), and the White Swan (No. 49). A number of grand Baroque palaces include Thun Hohenstein (No. 20) and Morzin (No. 5).

Italian Street ❼
VLAŠSKÁ ULICE

Map 3C.

Italian craftsmen, working on the Castle, settled here in the 16th century. The former Baroque Italian Hospital has an arcaded courtyard, but the grandest building is the former Lobkowicz Palace. One of Prague's finest Baroque palaces, it has a large oval hall on the ground floor leading out onto a magnificent garden. Look for the pretty stucco sign on the At the Three Red Roses house, dating from the early 1700s.

Church of St Nicholas ❺

KOSTEL SV. MIKULÁŠE

This is Prague's finest example of High Baroque. Begun in 1702 by acclaimed father-and-son architects the Dientzenhofers, the last touches were put to their masterpiece in 1761. The church's statues, frescoes and paintings are by leading artists of the day. Extensive renovation was carried out in the 1950s.

Altar Paintings *include this study of St Michael.*

The Curving Façade *is graced by several statues, including this one of St Paul (1710).*

The Baroque Organ *of 1746, below a fresco of St Cecilia, patron saint of music, was played by Mozart in 1787.*

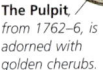

The Pulpit, *from 1762–6, is adorned with golden cherubs.*

Chapel of St Ann

VISITORS' CHECKLIST

Map 3C. Malostranské náměstí.
Tel 257 534215.
Open daily. Adm charge.
www.psalterium.cz

LITTLE QUARTER 49

A Fresco, The Celebration of the Holy Trinity, *fills the 70-m (230-ft) high dome.*

Dome

Clock tower

Chapel of St Francis Xavier

The Great Teachers *stand at the four corners of the crossing, including St Cyril dispatching the devil with his crozier.*

The High Altar, *surmounted by a copper statue of St Nicholas.*

View of the Little Quarter from the terrace of the Vrtba Garden

Vrtba Garden 8
VRTBOVSKÁ ZAHRADA

Map 3C. Karmelitská 25. Open daily Apr–Oct. Adm charge.

Behind Vrtba Palace is a beautiful Baroque garden (c.1720) with balustraded terraces. From the highest part of the Vrtba Garden there are magnificent views of Prague Castle and the Little Quarter. Statues of gods and stone vases are by Matthias Braun and paintings in the pavilion are by Václav Vavřinec Reiner.

Church of Our Lady Victorious 9
KOSTEL PANNY MARIE VÍTĚZNÉ

Map 4D. Karmelitská. Open daily. Free.

Prague's first Baroque building was the Church of the Holy Trinity (1613), later renamed after the Battle of the White Mountain. In the nave opposite Bernini's *Ecstasy of St Teresa* is the famed Holy Infant of Prague, its wax effigy enshrined in a glass case. It is one of the most revered Catholic images.

Maltese Square 10
MALTÉZSKÉ NÁMĚSTÍ

Map 4D.

The Knights of Malta once occupied this part of the Little Quarter, and the square still bears their name. It is dominated by the 12th-century Church of Our Lady beneath the Chain and such beautiful Baroque palaces as the Nostitz (c.1650) with its balustrade, statues and Classical vases. The attractive pink Rococo Turba (1767) was designed by Joseph Jäger.

Ferdinand Brokof's statue of John the Baptist in Maltese Square

Kampa Island 11
KAMPA

Map 4D.

In summer, locals sunbathe and sip wine in the delightful park at the southern end of the island. It is separated from the Little Quarter by the Devil's Stream (Čertovka), once home to a "laundry", milling area and, in the 1600s, a thriving pottery. It is known as "the Venice of Prague". Kampa's northern half is home to elegant embassies, restaurants and hotels.

LITTLE QUARTER

Grand Priory Square ⑫
VELKOPŘEVORSKÉ NÁMĚSTÍ

Map 4D.

On the garden wall of the Grand Prior of the Knights of Malta, graffiti artists have created a mural in memory of John Lennon. The doorways, windows and ornate vases – all by Matthias Braun – adorn the palace dating from the 1720s. On the opposite side of the square is the Baroque Buquoy Palace, almost contemporary with the Grand Prior's Palace.

Church of Our Lady beneath the Chain ⑬
KOSTEL PANNY MARIE POD ŘETĚZEM

Map 4D. Lázeňská. Open for concerts and services Sat, Sun. Free.

This church, the oldest in the Little Quarter, was founded in the 1100s. Its name refers to the chain used in the Middle Ages to close the monastery gatehouse. A Gothic presbytery was added in the 13th century, and two massive square towers guard the portico. In 1640 the church was given a Baroque facelift by Carlo Lurago.

Charles Bridge ⑭
KARLŮV MOST

See pp54–7.

Fresco that gave At the Three Ostriches its name

At the Three Ostriches ⑮
U TŘÍ PŠTROSŮ

Map 3D. Dražického náměstí 12.

Many of Prague's colourful house signs indicated the trade carried on within. In 1597 Jan Fux, an ostrich-feather merchant, bought this house by Charles Bridge. The plumes were very fashionable then with courtiers and officers at Prague Castle. In 1606 Fux rebuilt his house, adding a large fresco of ostriches. In 1714 Prague's first coffee house opened here. It is now a hotel and restaurant.

Čertovka (the Devil's Stream) with Kampa Island on the right

Bridge Street ⓰
MOSTECKÁ ULICE

Map 3D.

A major thoroughfare for 750 years, this narrow street linking Charles Bridge with Little Quarter Square is lined with Renaissance and Baroque houses. Look out for the Gothic tower in the courtyard of At the Three Golden Bells, the house At the Black Eagle for its rich sculptural decoration and splendid Baroque wrought-iron grille, and the ornate Rococo façade of Kaunic Palace.

Vojan Park ⓱
VOJANOVY SADY

Map 3D. U lužického semináře.
Open daily. Free.

A tranquil spot hidden behind high white walls, Vojan Park dates back to the 1600s, when it was the garden of the Convent of Barefooted Car-melites. Two chapels survive among the park's lawns and fruit trees. One is the Chapel of Elijah, in the form of a stalagmite and stalactite cave. The other chapel, built in the 18th century, is dedicated to St Theresa.

Kampa Museum of Modern Art ⓲
MUZEUM KAMPA

Map 4D. U Sovových mlýnů 2.
Open daily. Adm charge.

Housed in the Sova mill in the heart of Prague, this museum boasts an impressive collection of Central European art. Founded by a Czech-American couple to house their art collection, among works to be seen are those of abstract painter František Kupka and Cubist sculptor Otto Gutfreund.

Ledebour Garden ⓳
LEDEBURSKÁ ZAHRADA

Map 2D. Valdštejnská.
Open daily Apr–Oct. Adm charge.

Three gardens – dating from the 1700s and belonging to the former Ledebour, Pálffy and Černín Palaces – delight visitors with their elegant landscaping, attractive plants and magnificent views of Prague. The Ledebour has a fine pavilion and the Pálffy has terraces and loggias, but the most beautiful and architecturally the richest is the Kolowrat-Černín Garden.

18th-century statue of Hercules located in the Ledebour Garden

Observation Tower ⓴
PETŘÍNSKÁ ROZHLEDNA

Map 4B. Petřín. Open daily Apr–Oct, Dec; open Sat, Sun from Jan–Mar, Nov. Adm charge.

The most conspicuous landmark in Petřín Park is an imitation Eiffel Tower, but at 60 m (200 ft) the octagonal tower is a quarter of the height. The spiral staircase of 299 steps leads up to the viewing platform. On a

LITTLE QUARTER

The Observation Tower, built in 1891, overlooking the city

clear day you can see Bohemia's highest peak – Sněžka – 150 km (100 miles) to the northeast.

Mirror Maze
BLUDIŠTĚ NA PETŘÍNĚ

Map 4B. Petřín. Open daily Apr–Oct, Dec; open Sat, Sun from Jan–Mar, Nov. Adm charge.

The maze, with its walls lined with distorting mirrors, is in a wooden pavilion in the shape of the old Špička Gate, part of the Gothic fortifications of Vyšehrad. After navigating the maze, you can view the vivid diorama of *The Defence of Prague against the Swedes*, which took place in 1648.

Church of St Lawrence
KOSTEL SV. VAVŘINCE

Map 4B. Petřín. Closed to the public.

According to legend, the church was founded in the 10th century on the site of a pagan shrine. The sacristy's ceiling is decorated with a painting illustrating this legend. It dates from the 1700s when the Romanesque church was rebuilt featuring a cupola flanked by two onion-domed towers.

Observatory
HVĚZDÁRNA

Map 5C. Petřín 205. Open Tue–Sun year-round. Adm charge.

Since 1928, Prague's amateur astronomers have enjoyed the facilities of this observatory on Petřín Hill. You can use its telescopes to view the craters of the moon or distant galaxies. There is an exhibition of old astronomical instruments, and special events for children are held on Saturdays and Sundays.

Diorama of The Defence of Prague against the Swedes *in the Mirror Maze*

Charles Bridge (Little Quarter Side) ⑭
KARLŮV MOST

Prague's most familiar monument spectacularly connects the Old Town with the Little Quarter, across the River Vltava. Though now pedestrianized, at one time it could take four carriages abreast. Today, due to wear and tear, many of the 30 statues of saints are copies.

St Adalbert, 1709, *Bishop of Prague, founded the Church of St Lawrence on Petřín Hill in 991.*

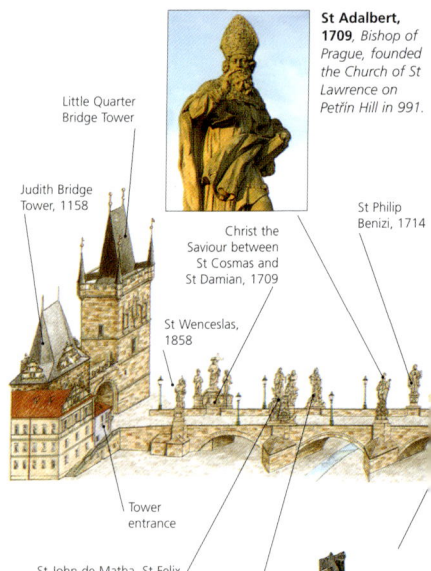

Little Quarter Bridge Tower

Judith Bridge Tower, 1158

Christ the Saviour between St Cosmas and St Damian, 1709

St Philip Benizi, 1714

St Wenceslas, 1858

Tower entrance

St John de Matha, St Felix de Valois and the Beatified Ivan, 1714

St Vitus, 1714, *the patron saint of dancers, is often invoked against convulsive disorders.*

St Luitgard, 1710, *is regarded as the most artistically remarkable on the bridge. This statue is based on the blind Cistercian nun's celebrated vision, when Christ appeared and she kissed his wounds.*

LITTLE QUARTER

View from Little Quarter Bridge Tower *gives a superb vista of the city of 100 spires.*

St Vincent Ferrer and St Procopius, 1712, *shows a rabbi saddened by St Vincent's success in converting many Jews to Christianity. St Procopius is one of Bohemia's patron saints.*

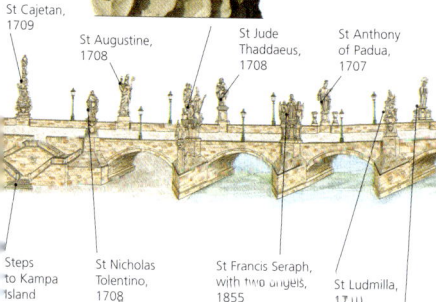

- St Cajetan, 1709
- St Augustine, 1708
- St Jude Thaddaeus, 1708
- St Anthony of Padua, 1707
- Steps to Kampa Island
- St Nicholas Tolentino, 1708
- St Francis Seraph, with two angels, 1855
- St Ludmilla, 1710

St John Nepomuk, 1683, *has been polished bright from people touching it for good luck.*

VISITORS' CHECKLIST

Map 4E. Little Quarter Bridge Tower open daily Apr–Oct. Adm charge. **www.prague-info.cz**

Charles Bridge (Old Town Side) ⓮
KARLŮV MOST

In 1357 Charles IV commissioned this Gothic style structure to replace Judith Bridge. The first statue (of St John Nepomuk) was added in 1683, inspired by Bernini's sculptures on Rome's Ponte Sant' Angelo. Usually crowded, the best time to see the bridge is at sunrise or sunset.

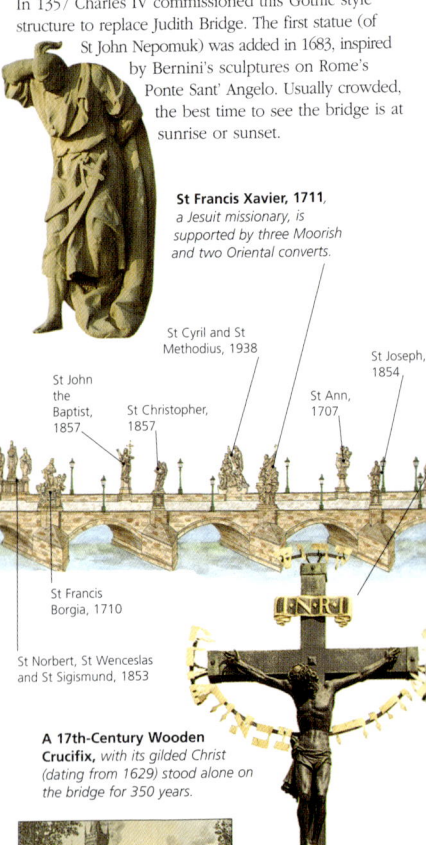

St Francis Xavier, 1711, *a Jesuit missionary, is supported by three Moorish and two Oriental converts.*

St Cyril and St Methodius, 1938

St Joseph, 1854

St John the Baptist, 1857

St Christopher, 1857

St Ann, 1707

St Francis Borgia, 1710

St Norbert, St Wenceslas and St Sigismund, 1853

A 17th-Century Wooden Crucifix, *with its gilded Christ (dating from 1629) stood alone on the bridge for 350 years.*

A Truce *with the Swedish army was signed on the bridge during the last hours of the Thirty Years' War.*

LITTLE QUARTER

The Madonna, St Dominic and St Thomas, 1708, *shows the Dominicans appearing with the Madonna and their emblem – a dog.*

Madonna and St Bernard, 1709, *depicts cherubs and symbols of the Passion.*

Old Town Bridge Tower

St Barbara, St Margaret and St Elizabeth, 1707

Pietà, 1859

St Ivo, 1711

Tower entrance

The Old Town Bridge Tower *is a Gothic structure built in the late 1300s. It was a fitting ornament and an integral part of the Old Town's fortifications.*

Pinnacled wedge spire

Roof viewing point

The Viewing Gallery, *a rib-vaulted room on the second floor, provides views of the Little Quarter.*

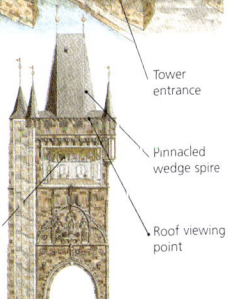

VISITORS' CHECKLIST

Map 4E. Old Town Bridge Tower open daily. Adm charge.

Nebozízek, the station halfway up Petřín's funicular railway

Hunger Wall ㉔
HLADOVÁ ZEĎ

Map 4B. Újezd, Petřín, Strahovská.

The fortifications built around the southern edge of the Little Quarter (on the orders of Charles IV in 1360–62) have been known for centuries as the Hunger Wall. Nearly 1,200 m (3,937 ft) of the wall, running from Újezd across Petřín Park to Strahov, survive with crenellated battlements and an inner platform for marksmen.

Petřín Park ㉕
PETŘÍNSKÉ SADY

Map 5C.

To the west of the Little Quarter, Petřín hill rises above the city to a height of 318 m (960 ft). In the 1100s the southern side of the hill was planted with vineyards, but by the 1700s most of these were transformed into gardens and orchards. Today a path winds up the slopes of Petřín, offering fine views of Prague.

Statue of Karel Hynek Mácha in Petřín Park

Funicular Railway ㉖
LANOVÁ DRÁHA

Map 4C. Újezd. In operation daily. Adm charge.

Built to carry visitors up to the Observation Tower at the top of Petřín hill, the funicular was originally powered by water. At the halfway station, Nebozízek, there is a restaurant with fine views of the Castle and the city.

Museum of Music ㉗
ČESKÉ MUZEUM HUDBY

Map 4D. Karmelitská 2, Praha 1, Malá Strana. Open Wed–Mon. Adm charge.

Housed in the former 17th-century Baroque Church of St Magdalene, the museum boasts a magnificent atrium. Exhibits show the diversity of popular 20th-century music from film, television, photographs and sound recordings. Other exhibits include handcrafted instruments and the history of musical notation.

LITTLE QUARTER

Michna Palace ㉘
MICHNŮV PALÁC

Map 4D. Újezd 40.

Around 1580 Ottavio Aostalli built a summer palace here on the site of an old Dominican convent. In 1623 it was rebuilt in the Baroque style, with magnificent gardens modelled on those at Versailles, but over time the palace and gardens became a ruin. After 1918 the palace was converted into a sports centre with a training ground in the old gardens.

Restored Baroque façade of the Michna Palace (Tyrš House)

STREET LIFE

RESTAURANTS

Palffy Palác
Map 2D. Valdštejnská 14.
Tel 257 530522.
Expensive
Fine dining establishment revels in its tattered splendour.

El Centro
Map 3D. Maltézské náměstí 9.
Tel 257 533343.
Cheap
The Spanish chefs get the paella just right.

Kampa Park
Map 4D. Na Kampě 8b.
Tel 296 826112.
Expensive
Top-rated riverside restaurant. Fusion cuisine and Continental classics.

U Patrona
Map 3D. Dražického náměstí 4. Tel 257 530725.
Expensive
The Continental and Czech cuisine will please gourmets; balcony overlooking Charles Bridge will delight romantics.

See p80 for price codes.

Nebozízek
Map 4C. Petřínské sady 411.
Tel 257 315329.
Expensive
Restaurant halfway up the Petřín funicular.

PUBS AND CAFÉS

U Kocoura
Map 3C. Nerudova 2.
Serves excellent Pilsner.

Café de Paris
Map 4D. Maltézské náměstí 4.
Good food and attractive patio.

Segafredo Espresso
Map 3D. Malostranské náměstí 4.
Conveniently situated pit stop.

Restaurant Čertovka
Map 3D. U lužického semináře 24.
Riverside patio setting.

SHOPPING

Obchod pod lampou
Map 2D. U lužického semináře 5.
Marionettes on sale.

U bílého jablka
Map 3B. Úvoz 1.
Adorable ceramic miniatures.

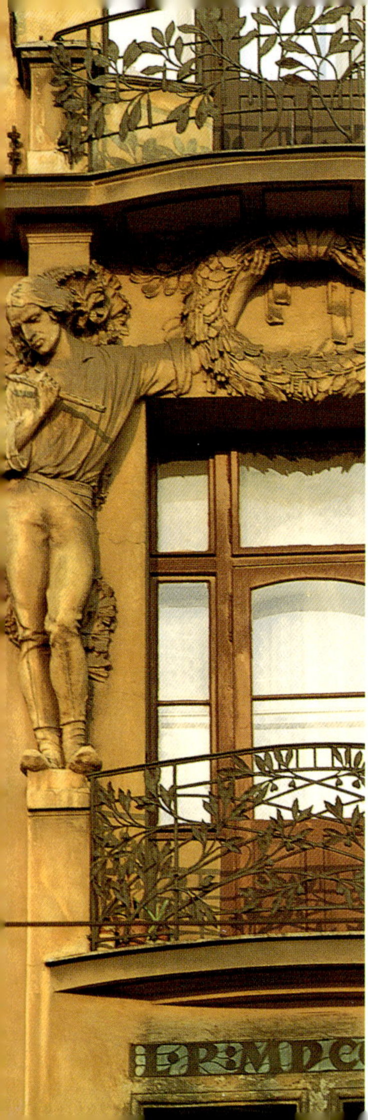

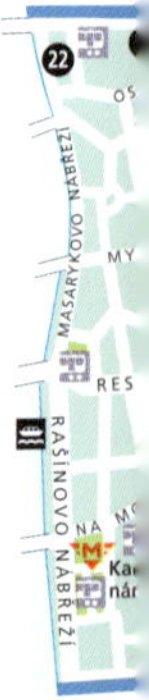
22
MASARYKOVO NÁBŘEŽÍ
RAŠÍNOVO NÁBŘEŽÍ

PRAGUE AREA BY AREA   61

NEW TOWN
NOVÉ MĚSTO

The New Town was laid out around three large central market-places: the Hay Market (Senovážné Square), the Horse Market (Wenceslas Square) and the Cattle Market (Charles Square). During the late 1800s much of it was torn down and redeveloped.

SIGHTS AT A GLANCE

Churches and Monasteries
Church of Our Lady of the Snows ②
Church of St Ignatius ⑧
Church of St Cyril and St Methodius ⑪
Church of St John on the Rock ⑬
Slavonic Monastery Emauzy ⑭
Church of St Catherine ⑯
Church of St Stephen ⑱
Church of St Ursula ㉑

Historic Buildings
Hotel Europa ④
Jesuit College ⑨
Faust House ⑫
New Town Hall ⑲

Theatres and Opera Houses
State Opera ⑥
National Theatre pp66–7 ㉒

Historic Squares
Wenceslas Square ①
Charles Square ⑩

Museums and Galleries
National Museum ⑤
Mucha Museum ⑦
Dvořák Museum ⑰

Beer Hall
U Fleku ⑳

Parks and Gardens
Franciscan Garden ③
Botanical Gardens ⑮

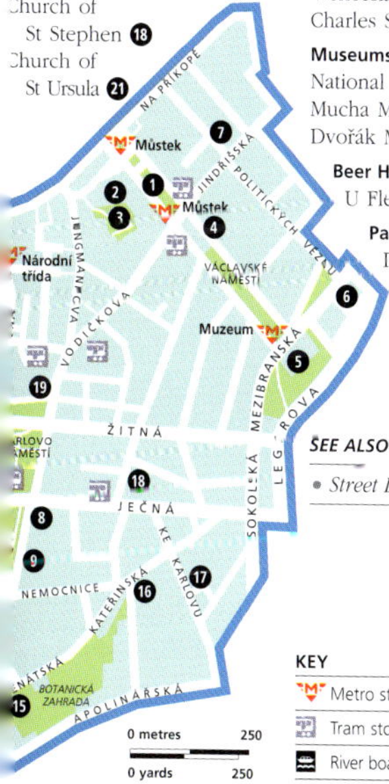

SEE ALSO
• Street Life p69

KEY
- Metro station
- Tram stop
- River boat boarding point

Sculptures on the Hlahol Choir Building on Masarykovo nábřeží

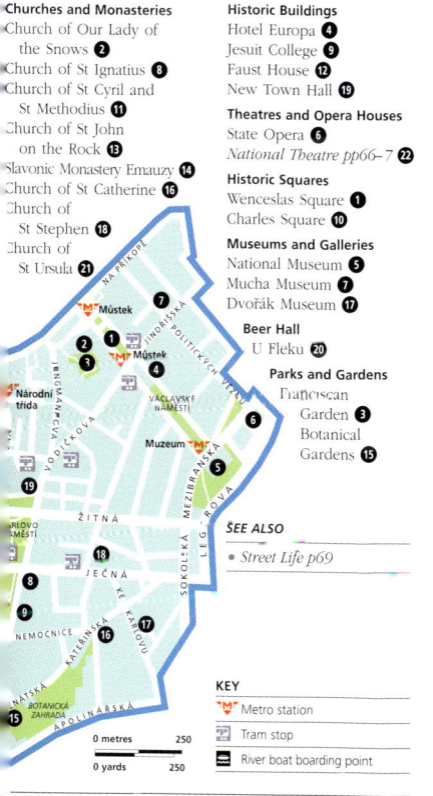

Wenceslas Square ❶
VÁCLAVSKÉ NÁMĚSTÍ

Map 4G.

The word "Square" is a little misleading, for this area is about 750 m (2,460 ft) long by only 60 m (197 ft) wide. Originally a horse market, today it is lined with hotels, restaurants and shops. The huge equestrian statue of St Wenceslas is by Josef Myslbek, the leading Czech sculptor of the late 1800s. At its foot are statues of other Czech patron saints.

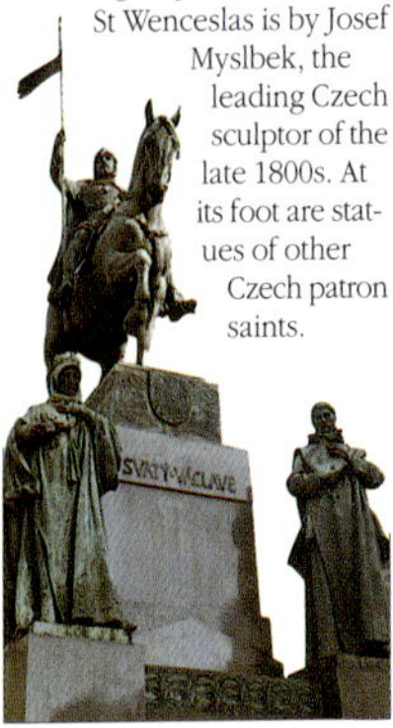

Wenceslas Monument in Wenceslas Square

Church of Our Lady of the Snows ❷
KOSTEL PANNY MARIE SNĚŽNÉ

Map 4G. Jungmannovo náměstí 18. Open daily. Free.

Over 33 m (110 ft) high, the towering building we see today is only a part of the huge church once envisaged by Charles IV. Inside, the intricate net vaulting of the ceiling dates from the early 1600s. Apart from the 1450s pewter font, the decoration is Baroque. The monumental three-tiered altar, crowned with a crucifix, is crowded with statues of saints.

Franciscan Garden ❸
FRANTIŠKÁNSKÁ ZAHRADA

Map 5G. Jungmannovo náměstí 18. Open daily. Free.

Originally constructed in 1348 by Charles IV, the garden was turned into a tranquil oasis close to Wenceslas Square by Franciscan monks in the 17th century. It was reconstructed between 1989 and 1992, when several of the beds were replanted with herbs once cultivated by the monks.

Hotel Europa ❹
HOTEL EVROPA

Map 5H. Václavské náměstí 29.

From the golden age of hotels, it was erected in 1889 and rebuilt in a highly decorated Art Nouveau style (1903–5). Not only has its splendid façade crowned with gilded nymphs survived, but many of the interiors on the ground floor have remained virtually intact, including the original mirrors.

Art Nouveau decoration on façade of the Hotel Europa

National Museum ❺
NÁRODNÍ MUZEUM

Map 5H. Václavské náměstí 68. Open daily (May–Sep: closed first Tue of month). Adm charge.

This vast Neo-Renaissance building (1891), designed by Josef Schulz, is at one end of Wenceslas Square. The entrance is reached by a ramp

NEW TOWN

Façade of the State Opera, formerly the New German Theatre

decorated with allegorical statues. Inside, collections include mineralogy, archaeology and natural history. From 2011 to 2014 exhibitions will be held in an adjacent building while the museum is renovated.

State Opera 6
STÁTNÍ OPERA

Map 5H. Wilsonova 4. Open for performances only.

A Neo-Classical frieze decorates the pediment above the columned loggia at the front of this theatre. The figures include Dionysus and Thalia, the muse of comedy. The interior is stuccoed, and original paintings in the auditorium and on the curtain have been preserved.

Mucha Museum 7
MUCHOVO MUZEUM

Map 4H. Panská 7. Open daily. Adm charge.

The 18th-century Kaunicky Palace is home to the first museum dedicated to this Czech master of Art Nouveau. Over 80 exhibits include paintings, drawings, sculptures, photographs and memorabilia.

Church of St Ignatius 8
KOSTEL SV. IGNÁCE

Map 6F. Ječná 2. Open daily. Free.

With its wealth of gilding and flamboyant stucco decoration, St Ignatius (built 1684–5) is typical of the Baroque churches created by Jesuits. The impressive interior is embellished with stuccowork and statues of Jesuit and Czech saints.

Main staircase of the National Museum

Sculptures on the façade of the Jesuit College by Tomasso Soldati

Jesuit College
JEZUITSKÁ KOLEJ

Map 7F. Karlovo náměstí 36. Closed to the public.

Occupying half the eastern side of Charles Square, this former Jesuit college was built by Carlo Lurago and Paul Ignaz Bayer between 1656 and 1702. The two sculptured portals are the work of Johann Georg Wirch. After 1773 the college became a military hospital. It is now a teaching hospital and part of Charles University.

Charles Square
KARLOVO NÁMĚSTÍ

Map 6F.

Since the mid-1800s the square has been a park. Though surrounded by busy roads, it is a pleasant place to sit and read or watch the world go by. The square was a vast cattle market, when Charles IV founded the New Town in 1348. In 1382, a wooden tower, which displayed the king's coronation jewels once a year, was replaced by a chapel

Church of St Cyril and St Methodius
KOSTEL SV. CYRILA A METODĚJE

Map 6F. Resslova 9. Open Tue–Sun. Adm charge for museum.

This Baroque church, with a pilastered façade and a small central tower, was built in the 1730s, then restored in the 1930s. Bullet holes, made by German machine guns during the siege of May 1942 by the Czech Resistance, can be seen below the memorial plaque on the outer wall of the crypt, which is now a museum.

Faust House
FAUSTŮV DŮM

Map 7F. Karlovo náměstí 40, 41. Closed to the public.

Prague thrives on legends of alchemy and pacts with the devil, and this Baroque mansion has attracted many alchemists. In the 1300s it belonged to Prince Václav of Opava, in the 1500s to Edward Kelley and in the mid-1700s, to Count Ferdinand Mladota,

Main altar in the Church of St Cyril and St Methodius

NEW TOWN

Baroque façade of Faust House

...whose chemical experiments gave rise to the legend of Faust.

Church of St John on the Rock ⓭
KOSTEL SV. JANA NA SKALCE

Map 7F. Vyšehradská 49. Open for services only. Free.

A small Baroque church (1738), this is one of Kilian Ignaz Dientzenhofer's most daring designs. Its twin square towers are set at a sharp angle to the church's narrow façade, a double staircase leads up to the west front and the interior is based on an octagonal floorplan.

Slavonic Monastery Emauzy ⓮
KLÁŠTER NA SLOVANECH-EMAUZY

Map 7F. Vyšehradská 49. Monastery church open Oct–May, Mon–Fri; Jun–Sep, Mon–Sat. Cloisters open by appointment. Adm charge.

The buildings (1347) have been altered many times during Prague's tumultuous history. In the 1700s the complex was given a thorough Baroque treatment; in 1880 it was rebuilt in Neo-Gothic style, and after WWII, the church gained a pair of modern concrete spires. The cloisters have some important 14th-century wall paintings.

Botanical Gardens ⓯
BOTANICKÁ ZAHRADA

Map 7G. Na slupi 16. Glasshouses and gardens open daily. Free (except for glasshouses).

Renowned for their rare plants, the gardens have been on this site since 1898, while the huge greenhouses date from 1998. Special botanical exhibitions and shows of exotic birds and tropical fish are often held here. Its star attraction is the water lily *Victoria cruziana*, whose huge leaves can support a child.

Entrance to the university's Botanical Gardens

Church of St Catherine ⓰
KOSTEL SV. KATEŘINY

Map 7G. Kateřinská. Closed to the public.

St Catherine's stands in the garden of a former convent (1354). In the 1500s it was rebuilt as an Augustinian monastery. In 1737, a new Baroque church was built, but it retained the slender steeple of the old Gothic church. Its octagonal shape gives it the nickname: "The Prague minaret".

National Theatre ②
NÁRODNÍ DIVADLO

This gold-crested theatre has always been an important symbol of the Czech cultural revival. The original Neo-Renaissance building of 1878 by Czech architect Josef Zítek was reconstructed by Josef Schulz after a fire in 1883. During the 1980s the theatre was restored, and the New Stage was built by architect Karel Prager.

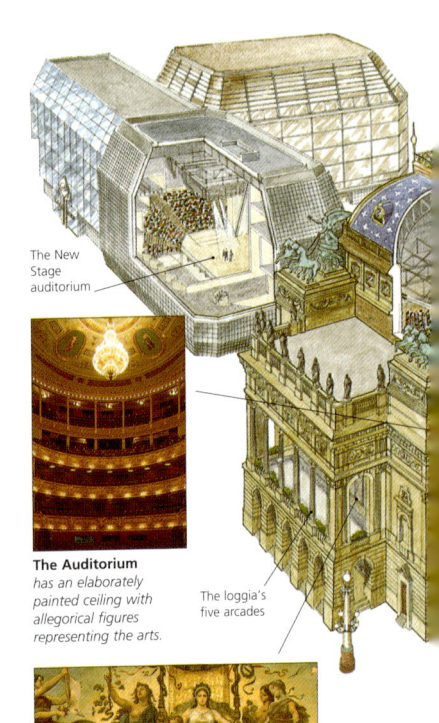

The New Stage auditorium

The Auditorium has an elaborately painted ceiling with allegorical figures representing the arts.

The loggia's five arcades

The Lobby Ceiling from 1878 has a fresco depicting the Golden Age of Czech Art.

NEW TOWN 67

The Stage Curtain depicts the theatre's origins.

This Figure, one of many representing the arts, stands on the western façade's roof.

The President's Box, lined with red velvet, is decorated with famous Czech historical figures by Václav Brožík.

VISITORS' CHECKLIST

Map 5E. Národní 2, Nové Město. Tel 224 901448. Auditorium open only during performances. Guided tours 8.30–11am Sat, Sun (Tel: 221 714151).
www.prague-info.cz

Dvořák Museum [17]
MUZEUM ANTONÍNA DVOŘÁKA

Map 7G. Ke Karlovu 20. Open Tue–Sun and for concerts. Adm charge.

One of the most enchanting buildings of the Prague Baroque, this red and ochre villa displays Dvořák's scores, plus photographs and memorabilia, including his piano, viola and desk. The two-storey house has a tiered mansard roof, a fine iron gateway, garden statuary by Matthias Braun and the ceiling and walls on the first floor are decorated with 18th-century frescoes by Jan Ferdinand Schor.

The Michna Summer Palace, home of the Dvořák Museum

Church of St Stephen [18]
KOSTEL SV. ŠTĚPÁNA

Map 6G. Štěpánská. Open only for Sun services. Free.

Built in 1351 with its multi-spired steeple, St Stephen's was re-Gothicized in the 1870s by Josef Mocker. Among its fine Baroque paintings are *The Baptism of Christ* by Karel Škréta and one of St John Nepomuk by Jan Jiří Heinsch. Its greatest treasure is a beautiful Gothic panel painting of the Madonna, known as *Our Lady of St Stephen's* dating from 1472.

Gothic pulpit in St Stephen's

New Town Hall [19]
NOVOMĚSTSKÁ RADNICE

Map 6F. Karlovo náměstí 23. Tower open May–Sep, Tue–Sun. Adm charge.

The New Town Hall dates from the 1300s, its Gothic tower added in the mid-1400s. In the 1500s it acquired an arcaded courtyard. After Prague's four towns joined up in 1784, it ceased to be a seat of administration. It is now used for cultural and social events, and often for wedding receptions.

Renaissance painted ceiling in the New Town Hall

U Fleků [20]

Map 6F. Křemencova 11. Museum open Tue–Sat.

This archetypal Prague beer ha (dating from 1499) has kept u

U Fleků, Prague's best-known beer hall

the tradition of brewing as an art. In 1762 the brewery was purchased by Jakub Flekovský, who named it U Fleků (At the Fleks). Today's brewery, the smallest in Prague, makes a special strong, dark beer, sold only here. There is also a museum of Czech brewing history.

Church of St Ursula ㉑
KOSTEL SV. VORŠILY

Map 5F. Ostrovní 18. Closed for renovation.

The original sculptures of 1672 still decorate the façade of this Baroque church. Statues featuring St John Nepomuk (1747) are in front. Unusually, the side of the church faces the street due to a lack of space when it was built. The airy interior has a frescoed, stuccoed ceiling and lively Baroque paintings.

National Theatre ㉒
NÁRODNÍ DIVADLO

See pp66–7.

STREET LIFE

RESTAURANTS

Dynamo
Map 6F. Pštrossova 29.
Tel 224 932020.
Moderate
Serves dishes such as marinated tongue in black sauce.

Celeste Restaurant
Map E6. Rašínovo nábřeží 80.
Tel 221 984160.
Expensive
French cuisine and stunning views in Gehry and Milunić's famous "Dancing House".

Jan Paukert
Map E5. Narodni trida 17.
Cheap
Historic deli and cafeteria known for its Czech open sandwiches and great cakes.

Zahrada v opeře
Map 6H. Legerova 75.
Tel 224 239685.
Moderate
The perfect gourmet dinner choice. Outstanding value.

PUBS AND CAFÉS

U Fleků
Map 6F. Křemencova 11.
Prague's most popular beer hall among tourists.

Globe
Map 5F. Pštrossova 6.
Bookstore and coffee shop in a historic building.

Radost FX Café
Map 6H. Bělehradská 120.
Casual atmosphere and decent vegetarian food.

Bar 02
Map 6F. Karlovo náměstí.
A former public toilet transformed into a pub with a fun rooftop patio.

U Havrana
Map 6F. Hálkova 6.
Goulash, fried cheese and great beers are served here until the early hours.

See p80 for price codes.

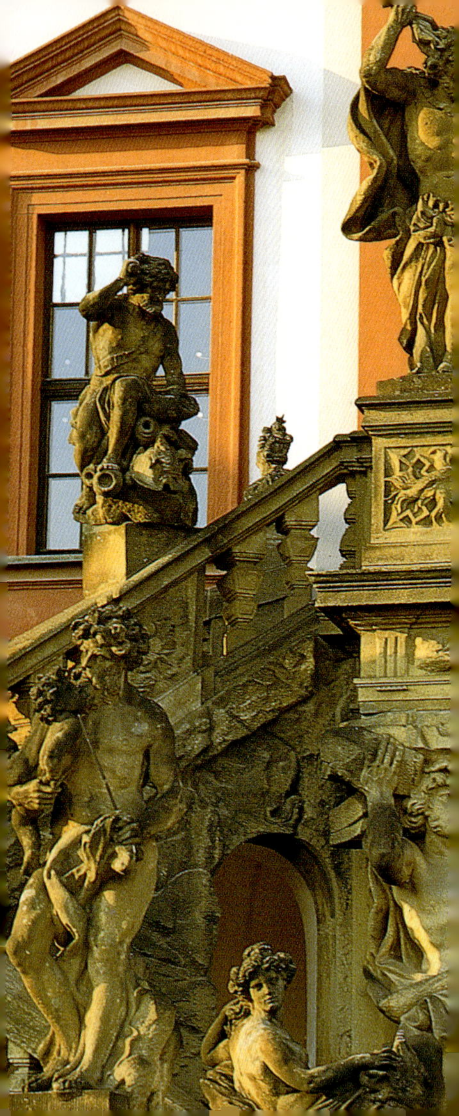

: PRAGUE AREA BY AREA

FURTHER AFIELD

Visitors to Prague, finding the heart of the city packed with sights, tend to ignore the suburbs, but it is well worth exploring outside the centre. Most of the museums and other sights in this section are easily reached by Metro, tram or even on foot. If you are prepared to venture a little further, the grand palace at Troja or the former monastery at Zbraslav, which houses the National Gallery's Asian Art collection, are not to be missed.

SIGHTS AT A GLANCE

Museums and Galleries
Mozart Museum ❶
Prague Museum ❸
National Technical Museum ❹
Trades Fair Palace ❺
Zbraslav Monastery ❿

Monasteries
Břevnov Monastery ❾

Cemeteries
Olšany Cemeteries ❷

Historic Buildings
Troja Palace ❼

Parks and Gardens
Exhibition Ground and Stromovka Park ❻
Zoo ❽

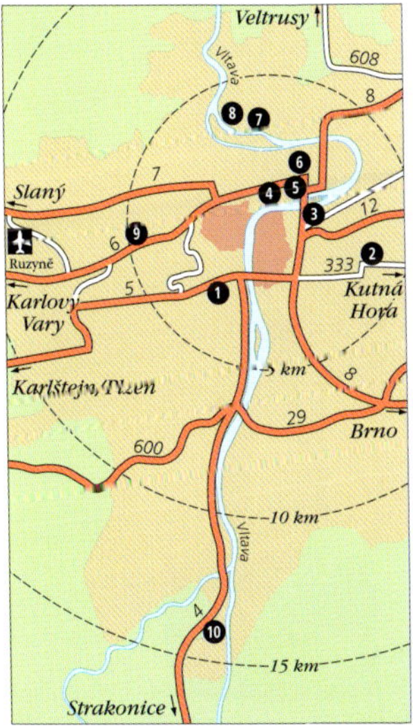

15 km = 10 miles

KEY

✈ Airport

◀ *Part of the garden staircase at the 17th-century Troja Palace*

Bertramka, the villa that houses the Mozart Museum

Mozart Museum ①
BERTRAMKA

Mozartova 169. Open daily. Adm charge.

Mozart stayed in this 17th-century farmhouse when he was working on *Don Giovanni*. It has a small Mozart exhibition.

Olšany Cemeteries ②
OLŠANSKÉ HŘBITOVY

Vinohradská 153, Jana Želivského. Open daily. Free.

The cemeteries, including a Jewish and a Russian cemetery and one from 1679 for plague victims, contain tombs for Franz Kafka and painter Josef Mánes.

Well-tended grave in the eastern part of the Olšany Cemeteries

Prague Museum ③
MUZEUM HLAVNÍHO MĚSTA PRAHY

Na Poříčí 52. Open Tue–Sun. Adm charge.

Stucco and sculptures decorate the Neo-Renaissance façade. Paintings, china and furniture are on display, but the most remarkable exhibit is a paper and wood model of Prague.

National Technical Museum ④
NÁRODNÍ TECHNICKÉ MUZEUM

Kostelní 42. Reopens in autumn 2010 following renovation.

This houses Europe's largest collection of items from the Industrial Revolution to the present day, with locomotives, railway carriages, bicycles, motorcars and motorcycles.

Trades Fair Palace ⑤
VELETRŽNÍ PALÁC

Veletržní Palác, Dukelských hrdinů 47. Open Tue–Sun. Free.

The National Gallery's Centre for Modern and Contemporary Art displays a superb collection: from French 19th-century, Impressionists, Picasso and Klimt to Czech modern.

FURTHER AFIELD

Exhibition Ground and Stromovka Park ⑥
VÝSTAVIŠTĚ A STROMOVKA

Exhibition Ground open daily. Adm charge. Park open 24 hours daily. Lapidarium open Tue–Sun.

Exhibitions, sports and artistic events and a funfair are staged in the summer. The Lapidarium has a sculpture exhibition, and the wooded park is ideal for a walk.

The Industrial Palace, centrepiece of the 1891 Exhibition Ground

Troja Palace ⑦
TROJSKÝ ZÁMEK

U trojského zámku 1, Prague 7. Open Apr–Oct Tue–Sun; Nov–Mar, Sat, Sun. Adm charge.

This striking summer palace was modelled on a Classical Italian villa, and the magnificent interior is full of extravagant frescoes. Its landscaped garden was laid out in formal French style.

A terracotta urn on the garden balustrade at Troja Palace

A red panda at Prague Zoo

Zoo ⑧
ZOOLOGICKÁ ZAHRADA

U trojského zámku 3. Open daily. Adm charge.

Situated on a rocky slope over-looking the Vltava, the zoo's 5,000 animals represent 650 species, some of them extremely rare. Its breeding programmes include big cats and Przewalski's horses.

Břevnov Monastery ⑨
BŘEVNOVSKÝ KLÁŠTER

Markétská 28. Tours only, Sat, Sun. Adm charge.

Founded in 993, this was Bohemia's first monastery, but it was rebuilt in Baroque style. In 1964 the crypt of the original 10th-century church was discovered below the choir and is open to the public.

Zbraslav Monastery ⑩
ZBRASLAVSKÝ KLÁŠTER

Zámek Zbraslav. Monastery closed to the public.

In 1292 Wenceslas II founded a monastery as the burial place for royalty. It was destroyed by the Hussites in 1420, and the present Baroque complex dates from 1732. The unique sculpture gardens here remain open to the public.

Getting Around

The centre of Prague is conveniently small and most sights can be reached comfortably on foot. The public transport system is efficient, clean and cheap. One ticket covers the metro and trams for the city centre, as well as buses to the suburbs.

A sign showing a street or square name and district

On Foot

Walking is the most enjoyable way to see Prague, but with steep hills, cobbled streets and tram lines, flat, comfortable shoes are a must. At traffic lights cross only when the green figure is flashing. Note that drivers tend to ignore crossings without lights. Trams run in the centre of the road, in both directions. They travel fast, and may come upon you with little warning.

The Transport System

The best way to get around the city centre is by metro or tram. Rush hours are 6–8am and 3–5pm (Mon–Fri). Some buses to the suburbs only run during peak hours. From 1 July–31 August a summer timetable operates, with fewer trains, trams and buses running. The Muzeum and Můstek metro stations (7am–9pm daily) and Ruzyně Airport (7am–10pm daily) have information offices where English is spoken.

Buying a Ticket

Purchase a ticket before travelling, then punch or stamp it in the machines provided. Buy single-ride tickets from tabák stores, metro stations or the bus driver, using exact change. Charges vary for the type of journey: up to 20 minutes on buses and trams with no transfer options (or five stops not exceeding 30 minutes on the metro), or up to 75 minutes, including a route change. Children under six travel free and 6- to 15-year-olds travel half price. You can also buy network tickets *(síťová jízdenka)* valid for unlimited rides on buses, trams and metro from 24 hours to 30 days.

The Metro

Metro entrances have green signs displaying an arrow pointing downwards. Buy a ticket, then take an

The green metro sign for Můstek metro station

GETTING AROUND

Central corridor with platforms either side and signs indicating direction of trains

escalator down to the platforms. Train directions are shown on signs hanging from the ceiling. On board the name of the next station is announced in Czech. Maps of the metro system are located above each door. Line A covers the city centre's main areas.

Trams

Trams run every 10 to 20 minutes (every 30 minutes after the metro closes). Each stop has a timetable: the stop underlined is where you are waiting; stops below that line tell where the tram is heading. Buy a ticket before boarding, then insert it into a machine inside the door to validate it. Doors open or close automatically, or you must push a button. Each stop is announced.

Buses

Buy a ticket before boarding, then validate it on entering. Doors open and close automatically; the end of the boarding period is signalled by a high-pitched sound. A single-journey ticket is only valid for that journey. Bus frequency varies according to the time of day. Through the night there are 13 bus routes that go to the outer areas not served by the tram and metro system.

Taxis

Taking taxis can be a very expensive way of getting around Prague. Always negotiate a fare you think is reasonable before you enter the cab. Taxi drivers speak only basic English, so communication can be difficult. It can be helpful to write down your destination in Czech. At night, charges increase, sometimes by 200 or even 300 per cent. Be sure surcharges are included in the figure you negotiate beforehand.

One of central Prague's many taxi ranks

Driving a Car

Prague's complex web of one-way streets, the many pedestrianized areas and a severe shortage of parking spaces can make driving very difficult and frustrating. You are better off taking public transport.

Survival Guide

Prague is still safer than most Western cities, despite a small increase in petty crime. This section includes information on money, making phone calls or sending postcards, dealing with medical or dental emergencies and the police.

The ornately decorated façade of a typical Prague bank

MONEY

Currency
The crown (Kč) is the Czech Republic's currency. Crown notes come in Kč5,000, Kč2,000, Kč1,000, Kč500, Kč200, Kč100 and Kč50 denominations. Coins are: Kč1, Kč2, Kč5, Kč10, Kč20 and Kč50. Prices may still be given in the now defunct heller (one-hundredth of a crown) – round these to the nearest crown.

Banks
Most banks are open from 8am to 5pm. Some, like Živnostenská banka, are worth visiting for their stunning interiors. Also, Prague banks charge lower fees for currency exchange than bureaux de change and hotels in the city.

ATMs
Bankomats are widely available throughout the city centre. Most machines recognize major credit cards and global systems like Cirrus. Be vigilant when using ATMs after dark.

COMMUNICATIONS

Telephones
When not out of order, payphones accept either coins or phone cards *(telefonni karty)*. These are available at newsagents, post offices and supermarkets. More than 70 per cent of Czechs have mobile phones. You can rent one at Prague's Ruzyně airport.

Post
The main post office (at Jindřišská 14, just off Wenceslas Square) is open from 2am to midnight. It is lovely inside and worth a visit, even if you don't need to mail a postcard or letter overseas. It also offers a money-wiring service.

A post office sign

Internet
As in most cities, nowadays you can find an Internet café on almost any corner. Expect to be charged upwards of Kč60 an hour, with a minimum time of 15 minutes. Many visitors do their surfing at The Globe (Pštrossova 6).

SURVIVAL GUIDE

HEALTH

Hospitals
More doctors speak English now and are accustomed to Western standards of care. Some private clinics, catering for foreigners, such as the Canadian Medical Centre (Veleslavínská 30; Tel 235 360 133), have doctors on call 24 hours a day. For in-patient care, go to the clinic for foreigners at Na Homolce Hospital (Roentgenova 2; Tel: 257 272 146).

Dentists
Czech dental care is among the best in Europe. English-speaking dentists at the American Dental Associates (V Celnicí 4; Tel: 221 181 121) or Millennium Dental Care Centre (V Celnicí 10; Tel: 221 033 405) are fine for routine care. For an emergency, call 224 946 981.

Pharmacies
For common medicines like aspirin or cold remedies, you must go to a lékárna. A pharmacy at the Kotva department store (Náměstí Republiky 8) is open at weekends, but most are closed. There are others scattered around, plus a few 24-hour pharmacies, including one at Palackého 5; Tel: 224 946 982.

SAFETY

Police
Visitors find Prague's municipal police helpful, although they continue to be dogged with accusations of bribe-taking. Don't confuse members of private security services and Prague Castle guards for state or municipal police officers.

EMERGENCY NUMBERS

Ambulance
Rychlá lékařská pomoc
Tel: 155

Police
Tísňové volání policie
Tel: 158

Fire
Tísňové volání hasičů
Tel: 150

Emergency Operator
Tel: 112 (in English)

MEDICAL CENTRES

Diplomatic Health Centre
Nemocnice Na Homolce
Roentgenova 2.
Tel: 257 272 146

First Aid/Emergency Dental Care
Nemocnice Na Františku
Palackého 5. Open: 7pm–6:30am Mon–Thu, 4pm–6:30am Fri, 6:30am–6:30pm, 7pm–6:30am Sat, Sun;
Tel: 224 946 981

General Health Care Corporation
Krakovská 8.
Tel: 222 211 206

24-hour Pharmacy
Palackého 5.
Tel: 224 964 982

A pharmacy sign

Index

Archbishop's Palace 38
Art Nouveau 5, 7, 26, 62, 63
At the Black Eagle 52
At the Fleks 69
At the Franciscans 62
At the Golden Well 46
At St Thomas's 46
At the Three Golden Bells 73
At the Three Ostriches 51
At the Three Red Roses 47
At the Two Suns 47

Ball Game Hall 35
bars *see* pubs, bars and cafés
beer halls 46, 68
Belvedere 7, 35
Bertramka 72
Botanical Gardens 65
Břevnov Monastery 73
Bridge Street 52
Buquoy Palace 51

cafés *see* pubs, bars and cafés
Capuchin Monastery 42
Carolinum 11
Černín Palace 42, 52
Chapel of Elijah 52
Chapel of St Theresa 52
Chapel of St Wenceslas (St Vitus's Cathedral) 6, 32
Charles Bridge 4, 45, 51, 52, 54–57
Charles Square 64
Charles Street 16
Charles University 64
Clam-Gallas Palace 13, 16
Clementinum 16, 17
Convent of the Barefooted Carmelites 52
Cubist Houses 26

Dalibor Tower (Prague Castle)
Devil's Stream 50, 51
Dvořák Hall (Rudolfinum) 20
Dvořák Museum 68

Estates Theatre 10
Exhibition Ground 73

Faust House 64, 65
Franciscan Garden 62
Funicular Railway 58

Garden on the Ramparts 34
Golden Horseshoe 47
Golden Lane (Prague Castle) 30, 31
Grand Priory Square 51

Hartig Garden 34
High Synagogue 6, 21
Hlahol Choir Building 61
Holy Ghost, Church of the 21
Holy Saviour (Clementinum), Church of the 16, 17
Hotel Europa 7, 62
House at the Golden Snake 16
House at the Two Golden Bears 12
Hunger Wall 58

Industrial Palace 73
Italian Hospital 47
Italian Street 47

Jesuit College 64
Jewish Burial Society 20
Jewish Museum 6
see under High, Klausen, Maisel, Old-New, Pinkas and Spanish Synagogues
Jewish Town Hall 21

Kaiserstein Palace 47
Kampa Island 50, 51
Kampa Museum of Modern Art 7
Kaunic Palace 52
Kaunicky Palace 63
Kinský Palace 6, 11
Klausen Synagogue 6, 20, 22
Knights of the Cross Square 17
Kolowrat-Černín Garden 52
Kučera Palace 42

Ledebour Palace and Garden 35
Lichtenstein Palace 47
Little Quarter Bridge Tower 45, 55

Little Quarter Square 47, 52
Little Quarter Town Hall 47
Lobkowicz Palace (Prague Castle) 34, 47
Loreto, The 6, 36–37, 42

Maisel Synagogue 6, 21
Maltese Square 50
Mariánské Square 16
Martinic Palace 39
Michna Palace 59
Michna Summer Palace 68
Mirror Maze 53
Morzin Palace 47
Mozart Museum 7
Mucha Museum 7, 63
Municipal House 7, 9, 10
Museum of Decorative Arts 7, 20, 23
Museum of Music 58
Museum of Physical Culture and Sport 59

Na Františku Hospital 26
Náprstek Museum 13
National Gallery 6, 27, 31, 38, 39, 72
see under Kinský Palace, St Agnes of Bohemia Convent St George's Convent, Sternberg Palace, Veletržní Palace and Zbraslav Monastery
National Museum 6, 34, 62, 63
National Technical Museum 72
National Theatre 66–67
Nativity, Church of the 37
Nebozízek station 58
Nerudova Street 47
New Town 68
New World 39
Nostitz Palace 50

Observation Tower 52, 53, 58
Observatory 53
Old Jewish Cemetery 6, 19, 22–23

INDEX

Old-New Synagogue 6, 24–25
Old Town Bridge Tower 17, 57
Old Town Hall 14–15
Old Town Square 5, 11
Olšany cemeteries 72
Our Lady Queen of Angels (Capuchin), Church of 42
Our Lady (Strahov), Church of 40
Our Lady before Týn, Church of 11
Our Lady beneath the Chain, Church of 50, 51
Our Lady of the Snows, Church of 62
Our Lady Victorious, Church of 50

Palace of the Lords of Kunštát 16
Pálffy Palace and Garden 52
Paradise Garden 34
Petřín Hill 53, 58
Petřín Park 7, 52, 58
Picture Gallery of Prague Castle 6, 30
Pinkas Synagogue 6, 20, 22
Pohořelec 42
Powder Gate 10
Powder Tower (Prague Castle) 30
Prague Castle 4, 6, 7, 29, 30, 34, 35, 38, 43, 46, 47
  Dalibor Tower 34
  Golden Lane 30, 31
  Lobkowicz Palace 34, 47
  Picture Gallery of 6, 30
  Powder Tower 30
  Riding School 38
  Royal Palace and Garden 7, 30, 35
  St George's Basilica 30, 31
  St George's Convent 6, 31
  St Vitus's Cathedral 4, 5, 6, 30, 32–33, 38
  South Gardens 7, 34
Prague Museum 72
pubs, bars and cafés
  At St Thomas's 46
  in the Jewish Quarter 27

pubs, bars and cafés (cont.)
  in the Little Quarter 59
  in New Town 69
  in Old Town 17
  in Prague Castle and Hradčany 43
  U Fleků 68, 69

Red Eagle 47
restaurants
  At the Franciscans 62
  At the Three Ostriches 51
  Convent Restaurant 69
  in the Jewish Quarter 27
  in the Little Quarter 59
  in New Town 69
  in Old Town 17
  in Prague Castle and Hradčany 43
Riding School (Prague Castle) 38
Royal Palace and Garden (Prague Castle) 7, 30, 35
Royal Summer Palace see Belevedere
Rudolfinum 6

St Agnes of Bohemia Convent 6, 27
St Castullus, Church of 26
St Catherine, Church of 65
St Cyril and St Methodius, Church of 64
St Francis, Church of 17
St Gall, Church of 12
St George's Basilica (Prague Castle) 30, 31
St George's Convent (Prague Castle) 6, 31
St Giles, Church of 13
St Ignatius, Church of 63
St James, Church of 10
St John on the Rock, Church of 65
St Lawrence (Petřín), Church of 53
St Martin in the Wall, Church of 13
St Nicholas (Little Quarter), Church of 6, 48–49

St Nicholas (Old Town), Church of 12
St Simon and St Jude, Church of 26
St Stephen, Church of 68
St Thomas, Church of 46
St Ursula, Church of 69
St Vitus's Cathedral (Prague Castle) 4, 5, 6, 30, 32–33, 38
Santa Casa 36, 37
Schwarzenberg Palace 39
shopping
  in the Jewish Quarter 27
  in the Little Quarter 59
  in Old Town 17
Singing Fountain 35
Smetana Museum 6, 17
Smiřický Palace 47
South Gardens (Prague Castle) 7, 34
Spanish Synagogue 6, 26
Stag Moat 30
State Opera 63
Sternberg Palace 6, 38, 47
Strahov Monastery 6, 40–41
Stromovka Park 73

Thun-Hohenstein Palace 47
Trades Fair Palace 72
Troja Palace 71, 73

U Fleků 68, 69

Veletržní Palace 6
Vojan Park 52
Vrtba Palace and Garden 50
Vyšehrad 65

Wallenstein Palace and Garden 7, 46
Wenceslas Monument 62
Wenceslas Square 62
White Swan 47

Zbraslav Monastery 7, 73
Zoo 73

Acknowledgments

Dorling Kindersley would like to thank the following people whose help and assistance contributed to the preparation of this book.

Design and Editorial

Publisher Douglas Amrine
Publishing Manager Vivien Antwi
Managing Art Editor Kate Poole
Cartography Casper Morris
Design Pete Quinlan, Kavita Saha, Shahid Mahmood, Conrad Van Dyk
Editorial Emma Anacootee, Claire Baranowski, Hannah Dolan, Jude Ledger, Dora Whitaker
Production Controller Shane Higgins
Picture Research Ellen Root
DTP Jason Little
Jacket Design Simon Oon, Tessa Bindloss

Picture Credits

Every effort has been made to trace the copyright holders, and we apologize in advance for any omissions. We would be pleased to insert appropriate acknowledgments in any subsequent edition of this publication.

t = top; tl = top left; tc = top centre; tr = top right; cla = centre left above; ca = centre above; cra = centre right above; cl = centre left; c = centre; cr = centre right; clb = centre left below; cb = centre below; crb = centre right below; bl = bottom left; b = bottom; bc = bottom centre; br = bottom right.

The Publishers are grateful to the following individuals, companies and picture libraries for permission to reproduce their photographs:

ARCHIV HLAVHINO MESTA, PRAHY (CLAM-GALLASUV PALÁC): 56bl; CORBIS:© Royalty free 38b; www.czfoto.cz: Lubo Stiburek 75tl; Oldrich Karasek: 76br; Národní Gallerie V Praze: Oto Palan 27; NÁRODNÍ MUZEUM, PRAHA: 63br; MARION SUCHA: 47b.

JACKET
Front – CORBIS: Peter Adams t.
Back – DORLING KINDERSLEY: Rough Guides/Eddie Gerald t.

All other images © DORLING KINDERSLEY
For further information see www.DKimages.com.

Price Codes are for a three-course meal per person including taxes, extra charges and half a bottle of house wine
Cheap under Kč300
Moderate Kč300-Kč700
Expensive Kč700 or more

SPECIAL EDITIONS OF DK TRAVEL GUIDES

DK Travel Guides can be purchased in bulk quantities at discounted prices for use in promotions or as premiums. We are also able to offer special editions and personalized jackets, corporate imprints, and excerpts from all of our books, tailored specifically to meet your own needs.

To find out more, please contact:
(in the United States) **SpecialSales@dk.com**
(in the UK) **TravelSpecialSales@uk.dk.com**
(in Canada) DK Special Sales at **general@tourmaline.ca**
(in Australia) **business.development@pearson.com.au**

Phrase Book

In Emergency

Help!	Pomoc!	*po-mots*
Stop!	Zastavte!	*za-stav-te*
Call a doctor!	Zavolejte doktora!	*za-vo-ley-te dok-to-ra!*
Call an ambulance!	Zavolejte sanitku!	*za-vo-ley-te sa-nit-ku!*
Call the police!	Zavolejte policii!	*za-vo-ley-te poli-tsi-yi!*
Call the fire brigade!	Zavolejte hasiče	*za-vol-ey-te ha-si-che*
Where is the telephone?	Kde je telefón?	*gde ye tele-fohn?*
the nearest hospital?	nejbližší nemocnice?	*ney-blish-ee ne-mots-nyitse?*

Communication Essentials

Yes/No	Ano/Ne	*ano/ne*
Please	Prosím	*pro-seem*
Thank you	Děkuji vám	*dye-ku-ji vahm*
Excuse me	Prosím vás	*pro-seem vahs*
Hello	Dobrý den	*do-bree den*
Goodbye	Na shledanou	*na s-ble-da-no*
Good evening	Dobrý večer	*dob-ree vech-er*

Useful Phrases

How are you?	Jak se máte?	*yak-se mah-te?*
Very well, thank you.	Velmi dobře děkuji.	*vel-mi dob-rzhe dye kuyi*
Pleased to meet you.	Těší mě.	*tyesh-ee mye*
That's fine.	To je v pořádku.	*to ye vpo-rzhahdku*
Where is/are...?	Kde je/jsou ...?	*gde ye/yso ...?*
How long does it take to get to..?	Jak dlouho trvá se dostat do..?	*yak dlo ho to tr-va se do-stat do...?*
How do I get to...?	Jak se dostanu k ..?	*yak se do-sta-nu k ...?*
Do you speak English?	Mluvíte anglicky?	*mlu-vee-te an-glits-ki?*
I don't understand.	Nerozumím.	*ne-ro-zu-meem*
Could you speak more slowly?	Mohl(a)* byste mluvit trochu pomaleji?	*mohl- (a) bis-te mlu-vit tro-khu po-maley?*
Pardon?	Prosím?	*pro-seem?*
I'm lost.	Ztratil(a)* jsem se.	*stra-tyil (a) ysem se.*

Sightseeing

art gallery	galerie	*ga-ler-riye*
bus stop	autobusová zastávka	*au-to-bus-o-vah za-stah-vka*
church	kostel	*kos-tel*
garden	zahrada	*za bra-da*
library	knihovna	*knyi-bov-na*
museum	muzeum	*muz-e-um*
railway station	nádraží	*nah-dra-zhee*
tourist information	turistické informace	*tooristi-tske in-for-ma-tse*
closed for the public holiday	státní svátek	*staht-nyee svah-tek*